To dear Tony

Xxxxxxy

Haunted Houses, Ghosts & Demons

by
Roberts Liardon

Embassy Publishing
Laguna Hills, California

Unless otherwise indicated, all Scripture quotations are taken from the *King James Version* of the Bible.

Scripture quotations marked NIV are taken from the *Holy Bible, New International Version*. Copyright © 1973, 1978, 1984, International Bible Society.

Scripture quotations marked NKJV are from the *New King James Version of the Bible*. Copyright © 1979, 1980, 1982 by Thomas Nelson Inc., publishers.

Haunted Houses, Ghosts & Demons
ISBN 1-879993-15-5

Copyright © 1993 by Embassy Publishing Co.
P.O. Box 3500
Laguna Hills, California 92654

Published by Embassy Publishing Co.
P.O. Box 3500
Laguna Hills, California 92654

Contents

 **Roberts Liardon** was born in Tulsa, Oklahoma. He was born again, baptized in the Holy Spirit, and called to the ministry at the age of eight, after being caught up to Heaven by the Lord Jesus.

Roberts was powerfully commissioned by the Lord to study the lives of God's great "generals" — men and women of faith who were mightily used by God in the past — in order to learn why they succeeded and why they failed.

At age fourteen, Roberts began preaching and teaching in various churches — denominational and non-denominational alike — Bible colleges and universities. He has traveled extensively in the United States and Canada, and his missions outreaches have taken him to Africa, Europe, and Asia. Many of his books have been translated into foreign languages.

Roberts preaches and ministers under a powerful anointing of the Holy Spirit. In his sermons, Roberts calls people of all ages to salvation, holiness and life in the Holy Spirit.

Through Roberts' ministry around the world, many people have accepted God's call to yield themselves as vessels for the work of the Kingdom.

1

DEMONS ON THE RAMPAGE

Along a dark and lonely railroad track in a small North Carolina town, five or six students from a nearby college stand and wait for a ghost to appear.

They will not be disappointed.

It's approaching midnight when someone whispers excitedly, "Look! Do you see it?"

"Yes," the others answer in unison. "It's coming this way!"

Sure enough, about 100 yards down the track to the west, a faint glow has appeared on the tracks. It's not an approaching train. It seems to be someone walking toward them. Someone swinging a kerosene lantern.

The closer it gets, the brighter the light becomes, and the more definite the movement. Some of the students think they see a human form behind the light — at least the shape of an arm holding the lantern. It's coming closer...and closer...and then — it's gone!

The students are only mildly disappointed. They believe they've been in the presence of a ghost...and, for some of them, an unnatural appetite for supernatural things has been whetted.

Legend has it that the light that appears along this isolated stretch of railroad has to do with a brakeman who died here more than 100 years ago. There was a ghastly accident, the legend says, and the poor man was decapitated. Since then, he has come almost every night to walk along the railroad tracks near where he was killed.

That's what they say about this strange light. But what is it *really?*

In Pennsylvania, a young couple is ecstatic when they move into their new home. It's an old house that needs quite a bit of work, but it's in a terrific neighborhood and, really, just what they were looking for.

But soon after they move into the house, the couple's four-year-old son begins spending a lot of his time playing with an imaginary friend he calls "the old man." At first, the parents aren't worried because they figure it is common for children to play with imaginary friends.

But then strange things begin to happen.

The little boy refuses to come to dinner because he'd rather stay in the basement, playing with the old man. He becomes rebellious and more withdrawn from the family.

Sometimes a rocking chair in the living room starts to creak back and forth even though no one is in it.

The smell of pipe tobacco sometimes fills the air, although no one in the family smokes.

And sometimes, the family cat begins growling and hissing for no apparent reason, the fur stands up on the back of its neck, and it runs, terrified, from the room.

Then, one day, the father is raking leaves in the yard when he strikes up a conversation with one of the neighbors. He tells the neighbor all about "the old man," and the strange goings-on in their house. The neighbor is curious. Could the little boy give a description of this "imaginary" friend?

By the time the little boy finishes explaining what his new "friend" looks like, the color has drained from the neighbor's face and his hands are shaking.

The little boy, it seems, has given a nearly perfect description of the former owner of the house. An elderly and unhappy man who, unbeknownst to the little boy or his parents, had committed suicide in the basement of their new home.

Had the unhappy old man come back to haunt the place of his death? Or was something else at work in that old house in Pennsylvania.

What do you think about haunted houses and ghosts and such?

ARE THEY FOR REAL

I know, from experience, that they are quite real. There are ghostly beings walking our planet today...seemingly appearing and disappearing at will, rattling chains in the deep darkness of the night, sometimes moaning and groaning and scaring people half to death, and other times trying to win people over by showing their "wisdom" and "love."

But these are not ghosts...spirits of people who have died.

And even though a "haunted house" may be a scary place, the real work and aim of these "creatures of the night" is even more frightening. That's because wherever there is a manifestation of a ghost, you are really dealing with something much worse than disembodied spirits.

In any situation like those I've described above, you are dealing with demons — beings who are bound and determined to further the kingdom of their Lord and Master, Satan Himself.

Now if you talk about demons, most of the world will laugh at you. Even people who are willing to believe in ghosts may make fun of you if you believe in demons.

Intellectuals will tell you that demons don't exist. They'll say that the very term is a relic from a bygone age, when physical and mental illnesses were thought to be the work of supernatural forces. These days, they'll tell you, we know better. What used to be thought of as demons are really nothing more than the strange workings of the human mind and body.

But those intellectuals are wrong. Very wrong.

Those who are involved in the New Age Movement will also tell you that demons don't exist. They say that all supernatural forces are, by their very nature, good. But they, too, are very, very wrong.

Demons do exist, and they are doing everything within their power to destroy as many human souls as they possibly can. And now, as never before, demonic forces are on a rampage in this world. This is because they know they are about to be destroyed forever — that the rapture is right at the door and the thousand-year reign of Christ is drawing closer with every heartbeat — which means that their annihilation is also drawing closer. They are determined to take as many people into eternal destruction with them as is inhumanly possible.

All you have to do is look around you and you will see some areas where demons are hard at work:

•**Demons are rejoicing** over a job well done when teenage gangs take control of our city streets, and when kids no older than 13 and 14 years of age are committing murder and other violent crimes.

•**Demons are rejoicing** when the entertainment industry sells out to sex, violence and the degradation of the human spirit.

•**Demons are ecstatic** when America murders millions upon millions of innocent unborn children every year.

Those are only three obvious areas where demonic forces are at work in the world today.

As you can see, demons are involved in this world on a large, global scale, controlling politics, mass movements and even governments. They are also involved wherever possible, on a personal scale. Wherever a demon can find a way to gain entrance into a person's life, he is going to do his very best to gain total control over that person.

Demons may oppress and harass their human victims in

a variety of ways. They may impersonate dead loved ones. They may "haunt" houses or other places. They may rattle chains in the middle of the night, or make groaning noises, or seek to gain control over their victims' minds by pretending to be wise and benevolent spirits from a "higher plane." And they may also indwell or "possess" a person.

WHAT SHOULD MY RESPONSE BE?

But before we go any further, I want to make one thing as clear as I possibly can.

And that is: If you are a born-again, spirit-filled Christian, you don't have a single thing to fear from all the demonic forces in the world. It doesn't matter if every demon in the universe including Satan himself is lined up against you. If you have the power of Christ within you...if you are living for Him, and trusting Him, and taking delight in Him...all of the forces of hell are no match for you.

However, there is nothing to be gained by ignoring those demonic forces. You need to be aware that demons exist, and know what some of their tactics are, because you need to know how to overcome them. If you are a born-again and spirit-filled Christian, then sooner or later you are going to come face-to-face with demonic forces in one way or another, and when that happens, you need to know what to do.

You need to know how to use the authority you possess through Christ to overcome the forces of hell, to protect yourself and your loved ones from a Satanic onslaught, and to help others gain deliverance from the forces of evil.

I wouldn't suggest for a moment that any Christian should go around thinking about demons all the time. Our focus must be on the Lord, and not Satan. But at the same time, ignorance can be extremely dangerous. We *must* be aware of what Satan is doing in the world before we can combat it.

We need to understand that the satanic world has a government, a purpose, and a vision regarding what it seeks to accomplish. We need to know that Satan, who is also known as Lucifer, is as busy today as he has ever been, and that his one desire is for the destruction of all human beings, including you and me.

BE AWARE

In this book, I'm going to tell you who these demons are, what they want, and how to take authority over them.

Everything I say to you will be built upon the authority of God's Word, the Bible, and upon my personal experiences, which have validated the truths contained in the Scriptures.

By the time we're finished talking about demons, I want you to be so sure of your place in God, and so confident of His power in you, that you can turn into a mighty warrior at the first onset of any demonic confrontation. Perhaps you're a sweet little girl that everyone thinks of as oh-so feminine and not the least bit warrior-like. You can still have victory over all the forces of hell through the blood and power of Jesus Christ. Perhaps you're a businessman who wears a three-piece suit to work every day, and sits behind a desk. I want you to get to the point where you can recognize demon activity in the lives of your co-workers or your clients and deal with it, helping to set them free forever.

There are few things in this world that are sadder or more pathetic than someone who is held hostage by an indwelling demon. That person may go through life confused, not understanding why he does so many things that he doesn't really want to do, never realizing that it is the demon or demons inside of him that makes him act in such ways. Or, he may be well aware that he is demonized — he may hear voices and be subject to other strange phenomena — but simply doesn't know what to do about it. He doesn't understand that the power of Christ can set him free.

As I mentioned earlier, demons are very active in the world today, and if we choose to ignore them, we are giving them free reign to do whatever they want to do. Luke 4:18 tells us that one of the ministries of Jesus when He was here in the flesh was to "preach deliverance to the captives." Because we are commanded to follow in Christ's footsteps, we also need to be going about the business of "preaching deliverance," and setting free those who are held hostage by Lucifer and his armies from hell.

I don't expect you to go around *looking* for demons, but I do expect you to be able to deal with them swiftly, powerfully, and correctly when you do encounter them. And, as I said before, if you are doing your best to live for Jesus Christ, you *will* encounter them. I certainly have.

DEMONS IN CHURCH

For example, I will never forget a one-night meeting that I held in St. Louis. When I got up to preach, demons were the farthest thing from my mind. My intention was to talk about the glories of heaven — a nice positive message.

But half way through my planned sermon, the Spirit of God spoke to me: "I want to cast out devils tonight?"

What? I had been invited to talk about heaven. I wasn't sure how my hosts would react if I suddenly took an 180-degree turn and started dealing with hell, instead. But when God speaks, I listen, and obey. If God wanted me to cast out devils...and I was certain that He did...then I was going to cast out devils.

Well, it became apparent very quickly the reason why God wanted me to start dealing with demons. It was because there were so many of them in the auditorium. There were hundreds of people there, and most of them seemed to be accompanied by their own personal demons. I've never experienced another meeting like that one.

All of a sudden, it seemed like a wind swept into the room, and when it did, people all over began to react violently. Some yelled and screamed, some sobbed, others fell to the ground and rolled around, some slithering across the floor like snakes.

Suddenly, my attention was riveted on a big, burly man standing in the back of the room. He was glaring straight at me, with total hatred in his eyes. He didn't say it, but I knew what he was thinking: "I'm going to kill you!"

And then he was running right down the aisle, full-speed ahead, coming straight toward me.

There were a number of ushers in that auditorium, but nobody was about to get in the way of this huge, demon-filled guy, running as fast as he could down the aisle of this church, intent on killing anyone who tried to stop him. He had a long way to run, but as he came down the aisle one usher after another scrambled to get out of his path!

I was standing there, looking at him, bracing for the collision.

Now, behind me, on the stage, was another preacher who had been part of the program that night. He was not in the best physical shape. In fact, he was rather overweight. But he came running past me, jumped right off the stage (it was a fall of probably six feet or more, but he made the jump without even stumbling) and headed straight for the man who was heading straight for me. Well, I didn't care how big the demon-possessed man was, or how many demons he had in him — I knew he wasn't going to be any match for one overweight preacher with the power of God in Him. And sure enough, he wasn't.

That preacher made such a great diving tackle, you would have thought he was a lineman for the Dallas Cowboys.

Bam! The man hit the floor — cursing and growling and thrashing about the whole time. In a matter of minutes, several of the ushers had come out of their hiding places to help. All together, they grabbed the man, and held him up against the wall so they could minister to him. All the time they were casting the demon out of him, you could hear him screaming and yelling, and threatening to kill everyone in the room.

By the time they got him set free, he had actually left a huge dent where he had been banging his head against the wall — and it was a steel wall! That is the sort of thing a demon can do to a human being.

DEMONS ON A ROOFTOP

On another occasion, when I was living in Tulsa, Oklahoma, I got a call from a woman who was on the edge of hysteria. Her 14 year old son was totally out of control. He had become violent, having beaten his mother and thrown her into a corner. Then when his father tried to discipline him, the boy knocked the father to the ground and began beating him, too.

Now the father in this case was no wimp. He was probably an inch or two over six feet tall and looked strong enough to hold his own in any fair fight. But he was no match for his young son, who was not nearly as tall or as strong as his father was, but who had a supernatural strength due to the demons that had taken control of him.

When I got to their house, the parents told me that their son's abusive behavior had been going on for some time, and I could see that they were telling me the truth by the number of holes in the wall, the smashed lamps, and the numerous pieces of broken furniture.

This time, the attack had apparently been more severe than usual, and the mother was in the kitchen, whimpering and crying and shaking from fear.

As I walked into that kitchen, I felt the authority of God come on me. It came over the top of me and went down to the bottom of my feet. I felt like even my toes had power, and I knew there wasn't a power on earth that could stand against me.

"Where is he?" I asked her.

"He's on the roof."

Well, that's exactly where he was. Sitting up on the roof with a can of gasoline and a book of matches. He was pouring the gasoline all around him and threatening to set the house on fire.

"What are you doing up there?" I asked him.

"I'm trying to burn the house," he replied.

"Really?" I looked at him for a moment, and then said, "You're not going to do any such thing. You come down from there."

He just glared at me. "I'm not coming down."

"If you don't come down right now, I'm going to come up there and knock you off."

"You wouldn't dare."

He spit the words at me in a hate-filled challenge.

At this point, I should tell you that this all took place on a Sunday morning, and that I was wearing one of my favorite suits. At the moment, though, that didn't matter. I was going up on that roof to get that kid, and so that's what I did!

Only by the time I got up there, he climbed down just as fast as he could, ran into his bedroom and shut the door behind him. I followed him just as fast as I could, and when I got to his bedroom, he was lying in the fetal position in a corner, whining and moaning in a strange little voice.

He wouldn't turn around and look at me so I reached over and grabbed him and unwrapped him into the middle of the floor. At this point he went into a position that I can only describe as looking like he was being nailed to a cross, and he began to moan and scream, acting as if I were killing him.

But all I was doing was praying for him, laying hands on him and using the power of the name of Jesus and the weapons of our warfare. As I continued to pray for him, he began to growl...deep, guttural sounds like a dog about to attack. But I still wouldn't let go of him, and I wouldn't quit praying for him.

I kept on for about an hour, holding on tight and praying as hard as I could. I couldn't get him to look at me, and when I turned his head toward me to get his attention, he closed his eyes as tight as possible. But I wasn't about to quit on him.

It was quite a battle, but by the power of Jesus I was able to drive the demon out of him. Once I had done that, I still had the flesh to deal with. You see, one of the ways a demon can gain access into someone's life is when that person is lacking something and so has developed an unnatural craving for it. The evil spirit will oblige that craving by giving it a false sensation and satisfaction...and in this instance, what the boy was craving was attention and affection from his parents.

So even after the evil spirit was cast out of him, I still had to break the boy's fleshly pattern of behaving in a certain way so that he could be a normal son. And I also prayed for the boy's mother and father, that they would be able to deal properly with their son and feel free to show their love for him.

A few weeks later, that young man came to church where I was preaching, sat in the second row with his Bible on his lap, and took notes...and as far as I know, he's been a model citizen ever since. The difference between the first and second times I saw him was literally the difference between light and darkness.

It is truly amazing what the power of Satan can do to a

human being, but even more amazing to see the difference the power of God can make in a person's life.

The great preacher Lester Sumrall tells the story of what happened when he was conducting a crusade in the Philippines.

He was listening to the radio when an urgent appeal was made to anyone who could help a young girl who was in very desperate need. The announcer wasn't clear as to what was wrong with the girl, but the fear and urgency in his voice said that it was something terrible, and in the background, Brother Sumrall could hear the young girl screaming and carrying on the way you might expect from someone who was under demonic attack.

As he listened to the terrible wailing, he heard the Lord's voice saying, "Go and cast the devil out of her."

It wasn't something Brother Sumrall wanted to do, and he told the Lord so. "Please, Lord...let someone else cast the demon out of her."

The reply was not judgmental, but it was firm.

"You are the only one here who knows how to deal with this situation. Go!"

When God speaks to you like that, you have no choice but to obey, so Brother Sumrall went down to meet the girl and do as the Lord had commanded. It seems this young girl was serving time in a Philippine prison. She had been a prostitute, a drug-addict, and the Lord only knows what else. She had opened herself up to all sorts of evil influences, so it's easy to see how the demons had gained entry into her life.

When Brother Sumrall got to that prison, what he found was a young woman writhing and squirming in agony, panting and gasping for breath and — what was even more astonishing — teeth marks were suddenly appearing on the surface of her skin. Some unseen monster was actually attacking and biting the girl, and when it did she would scream and push at the air as if she was fighting to get something off of her, and she would scream, "They're biting me again!"

She was surrounded by reporters, doctors, witch doctors and priests, all of whom wanted to help the girl, but all of whom seemed to be completely helpless in the face of her agony. One of the reporters told Brother Sumrall that a couple of days earlier the girl had cursed two of her "enemies," and that they had died inexplicably the very next day. No wonder all of those who were standing around watching this pathetic scene were terrified!

It wasn't easy to get this girl free. Brother Sumrall cast the demons out of her by the power of Jesus...but because of the life she was living, and her reluctance to give her heart to Christ, even after He had set her free, they kept coming back into her. For three days in a row, Brother Sumrall had to go down to where she was, pray for her, get her to confess her sins, and cast the demons out of her yet another time.

Finally, on the day the spirits came out of her for good, he had everybody on their knees singing, "Oh the blood of Jesus." She was set free once and for all, and was able to get out of prison and live a happy and moral and Christian life thereafter. Well, you can do the same thing Lester Sumrall did. You have the same power within you that he had within him during those days in the Philippines *if* you belong to Jesus. And so, no matter what the demons may do, no matter how they may manifest themselves, you can defeat them through the power and blood of Jesus.

MULTIPLIED DEMONS

Before we move on to a discussion of who demons are and where they come from, let me give you one more example — this one from a secular source, *Time Magazine* of October 25, 1982. The article is titled, "The Twenty-Seven Faces of Charles." It tells the story of a young man, 29 years of age, who was found wandering in a dazed condition on the beach near Daytona Beach, Florida.

The paramedics who found him considered him to be retarded so they took him to the local hospital. At the hospital, the young man astonished doctors by speaking to them in two distinct voices. The first voice was that of a scared little boy who claimed that he was being abused. The second was that of an intelligent and articulate adult.

The young man was kept at the hospital for observation, and soon other "personalities" began to manifest themselves through him. He would sometimes snarl, growl, scream and curse violently. A Dr. Graham, who is described as the hospital psychiatrist, recorded more than 200 conversations with the young man, during which a total of 29 different entities spoke through him.

There was a young man named Mark, another one named Dwight, a blind mute called Jeffrey, an arrogant jock who said he was Michael, a woman named Tina, another female who said she was a lesbian, and a religious "mystic" who often spoke in terms associated with New Age philosophy. These different entities did not get along, would often fight each other, and one named T.K., who was especially angry, would sometimes do bodily harm to their host.

You can see from this that demons really are crazy. They are so full of hatred and anger that they can't get along with anyone or anything, including each other. They are united only in their hatred for God, their fear and contempt for the blood of Christ, and their desire to destroy the human race.

Now, of course, the doctors who dealt with this young man who had 29 different entities speaking through him would never tell you that he was possessed by evil spirits. They couldn't say that because they don't believe in demons. Instead, they have to talk in terms of split personalities and malfunctions of the brain. That's sad, because what is going on in the case of a young man like this, pure and simple, is that he has given demons entrance into his life and they are tearing him apart. He doesn't need a bunch of doctors sitting around and analyzing him, getting him to lie down on a couch and talk to them about his childhood. He needs an encounter with the blood of Christ, brought about by someone who is a born-again, Spirit-filled believer.

A few moments ago I asked you if you believe in ghosts, haunted houses and such. Now I have another question: Do you believe that demons exist? You should, because they are every bit as real as you and I. Whenever you hear or read of haunted houses and ghostly manifestations, you can know beyond any doubt that demons are involved.

The world doesn't understand this. The world talks of split personality or parapsychology or earth-bound spirits. And the world is ripe for seduction and betrayal.

There is a war raging on this planet. And whether you realize it or not, you are either on one side or the other. You are either fighting *for* God or you are fighting *against* God.

The truth is that all human beings who live on this planet are under attack. Isn't it way past time you started fighting back?

2

THE FALL FROM GLORY

We've already established that demons exist, and that they are bent on the destruction of mankind.

But where do they come from? Who created them? And who is their leader?

To find the answer to these questions we have to go way, way back into the mists of time, before the creation of man, and, in fact, even before God spoke this planet of ours into existence.

Sometime way back there, and we really don't know when, God created the glorious creatures called angels.

Chief among these were the archangels, including Gabriel, Michael, and another powerful being by the name of Lucifer.

Nobody knows for sure, but some speculate that Lucifer may have been the most powerful of all the archangels. Whether that is true or not, we know that he was an intelligent, beautiful and proud creature. He must have received a lot of recognition and praise from the other angels, and it went right to his head.

He became so puffed up with pride, in fact, that he decided he could do a better job of ruling the universe than God Himself. Apparently, some of the other angels felt the same way. Lucifer probably began to tell them what he would do if he were in charge, how he would make life better for them and, basically, planting the seeds of rebellion throughout the ranks of the angels.

How these angels ever thought they could actually

overthrow God is beyond my comprehension. Surely they knew there was really no way they could ever defeat him. It's also beyond my comprehension how they ever could have rebelled against God in the first place. After all, they lived so close to Him on a daily basis. They were first-hand witnesses not only of His amazing power, but of His overwhelming love for all of His creatures. It just shows you what a destructive force pride can be.

From certain Scriptures, we can ascertain that as many as two-thirds of the angels joined Lucifer in his rebellion. In a battle that raged throughout the universe, they were defeated, and banished from heaven forever. These fallen angels, then, are what we today know as "demons" or "devils." We sometimes get the idea that demons are hideous creatures, with ugly contorted faces, bat-like wings and horns growing out of the tops of their heads. That's hardly the truth. As I've already mentioned, Lucifer was a beautiful and powerful creature.

No wonder the Bible tells us that Lucifer is able to transform himself into an angel of light. In fact, his very name means "The Lightbearer." If he were an ugly and scary-looking thing, then no one would be attracted to him. But he is like sin. He looks pretty good until you get close enough to him that he can ensnare you.

Now when Lucifer and his followers were kicked out of heaven, that effectively sealed their eternal fate. When Christ rose from the dead following His crucifixion, that was the final nail being pounded into Lucifer's coffin. But for His own reasons, God has not yet destroyed Lucifer and his armies of darkness. And so even though they know they have been defeated, they are still carrying on their rebellion, still doing their best to be a source of irritation to God and His people. Lucifer himself is so deluded by his own power that he still believes he has a chance to wrest control of the universe away from God Almighty. As we look around us, it would seem that he can certainly take some fiendish pride in what he's able to accomplish on this planet, but whatever he is able to do here, it's only because his time of eternal destruction has not yet come — but, as I said in Chapter One, it is drawing very near.

In the 28th chapter of Ezekiel, we can get a glimpse of the nature of Lucifer and his rebellion against the Lord.

"You were in Eden, the garden of God;
Every precious stone was your covering;
The sardius, topaz, and diamond,
Beryl, onyx, and jasper,
Sapphire, turquoise, and emerald with gold.
The workmanship of your timbrels and pipes ·
Was prepared for you on the day you were created.

You were the anointed cherub who covers;
I established you;
You were on the holy mountain of God;
You walked back and forth in the midst of fiery stones.
You were perfect in your ways from the day you were created,
Till iniquity was found in you.

By the abundance of your trading
You became filled with violence within,
And you sinned;
Therefore I cast you as a profane thing
Out of the mountain of God;
And I destroyed you, O covering cherub,
From the midst of the fiery stones.
Your heart was lifted up because of your beauty;

"You corrupted your wisdom for the sake of your splendor;

I cast you to the ground,

I laid you before kings,

That they might gaze at you."

Ezekiel 28:13-17 (New King James)

We can see from this that Lucifer was a near-perfect creature. But he began to think he was responsible for his own power and beauty, and he wasn't responsible for it at all. God was. If we were to put it into the modern vernacular, we might say that Lucifer began to believe his own press releases. And it's a dangerous, dangerous game when you start to believe the good things that other people say about you.

For another biblical look at Lucifer, let's take a look at the 14th chapter of Isaiah, beginning with verse 12:

"How you are fallen from heaven,

O Lucifer, son of the morning!

How you are cut down to the ground,

You who weakened the nations!

For you have said in your heart;

'I will ascend into heaven,

I will exalt my throne above the stars of God;

I will also sit on the mount of the congregation

On the farthest sides of the north;

I will ascend above the heights of the clouds,

I will be like the Most High.'

Yet you shall be brought down to Sheol,

To the lowest depths of the Pit."

Isaiah 14:12-15 (New King James)

You see, when God created angels, He gave them free will to feel think and act for themselves. He did the same thing when He created human beings. He wants us to love and serve Him, not because we *have* to, but because we *want* to. If the angels had been robots, Lucifer never would have rebelled. If human beings had been automatons, Adam and Eve never would have eaten of the forbidden fruit in the Garden of Eden. But God has always believed in letting His creatures make their own choices about things, and in the case of Lucifer, his choice was to rebel. Notice how selfish Lucifer is when he says, "I will," "I will," "I will." In essence, he was praying, "Not Thy will, Lord, but mine be done."

Notice that Lucifer was not happy with who he was, with the way God made him. And so he said, "I will become like the Most High." In our world today, a lot of people are not happy with the way God made them. There are men who don't want to be men so they're having operations to turn themselves into women (although they're really not women, just mutilated men). And there are women who want to be men. There are black people who want to be white, and white people who want to be black, and all sorts of people who are flat-out unhappy with who they are. Such discontent always leads to trouble, and it is always right on the border of rebellion, shaking the fist at God and saying, "I could have done a better job than you did." It's just not so.

Let's take one more look at what the Bible has to say about Lucifer's fall from grace. This time, from the Book of Revelation, Chapter 12:

> **"His (Lucifer's) tail drew a third of the stars of heaven and threw them to the earth. And the dragon stood before the woman who was ready to give birth, to devour her child as soon as it was born." (Verse 4)**

The dragon in this verse is, of course, Lucifer, who did his very best to destroy the Christ child as soon as He was born. Remember how Herod ordered the killing of all male children under two years of age?

Let's go on further, reading verses seven through nine:

"And war broke out in heaven: Michael and his angels fought against the dragon; and the dragon and his angels fought, but they did not prevail, nor was a place found for them in heaven any longer.

So the great dragon was cast out, that serpent of old, called the Devil and Satan, who deceives the whole word; he was cast to the earth, and his angels were cast out with him."

THE GREAT TRICKSTER

Now I'm sure that most of us know the story of Adam and Eve, and how they fell from grace by disobeying God in the Garden of Eden. If you don't know the story, get your Bible, and turn to the third chapter of Genesis and read it to yourself. What happened here was that Lucifer used a talking snake to entice mankind into sin, thereby bringing sickness, disease and all sorts of terrible things into the perfect world God had created. This was the first encounter between Lucifer and humankind. That was thousands of years ago, but Lucifer is still using the same old tricks — still doing everything within his power to get you and me to turn away from God.

And if he can't do it subtly, by telling us lies and tempting us with tasty-looking sins, he'll do it by attempting to grab hold of us and taking control of our bodies and souls.

The greatest desire of any demon is to gain entrance into the soul, the spirit, the body of a human being and take up residence there. Gaining a victory like that over someone who has been created in God's own image (see Genesis 1:26-27) is a source of tremendous joy to one of these citizens of hell.

Please remember that it is not good to think too much about Lucifer or his demon armies. We don't want to give him too much credit, nor do we want to be focusing on him when we really need to keep our attention fastened on God, His Word and His glory. But at the same time, we need to know as much as we can about Lucifer in order to be able to fend off his attacks — in order to outsmart him. And one of the best ways we can learn about him is by going through the Bible and taking a look at some of the names it gives him.

SATAN HAS MANY NAMES

First of all, Ephesians 2:2 says that Lucifer is: **The Prince of the Air.**

According to Paul's writings, there are three heavens. The first in the earth's atmosphere, the second is the spirit world, or the heavens where there are spirit beings, and the third heaven is the planet called heaven — where all Christians are going to go eventually. The home of Lucifer is the second heaven, in the atmosphere of the spirit, and that's where he rules with his principalities. That is why he is called the "Prince of the Air."

The second name for Lucifer is: **The Prince of Darkness.**

This name is found in Ephesians 6:12. It's understandable that Lucifer would love the darkness because it helps to cover up his evil deeds. He's not the type of creature to be right out there in the bright sunshine because that would reveal him for who and what he is. And so he stays in the shadows, slinking around under the cover of the night.

Unconfessed sin is a type of darkness, and it will attract evil spirits. Hurts and wounds that have not been healed properly, that have not been dealt with by forgiveness, are a form of darkness, and they, too, will attract Lucifer and his armies.

If you are going to be strong, you must live in the light — the light of God's Word and the light of obedience to God.

Lucifer and his followers cannot stand the light, and they will flee from you.

Name number three? **Prince of This World.**

You'll find that reference to Lucifer in John 12:31 and again in John 16:11. That was a title he earned when he tempted Adam and Eve to turn away from God, and it is a title he will hold until the end times, when he will be thrown into the Lake of Fire, and utterly banished once and for all.

When Jesus Christ comes to rule and reign, He will be taking His rightful place as the king and prince of this world...but until that glorious day, Lucifer still has claim to much of this planet, as any news broadcast will show you.

Another name is **The Prince of Devils.**

You can find this name in Matthew 12:24, and this one is pretty obvious. But don't you think it would be terrible to be prince over a bunch of devils? I certainly do. You can bet that Lucifer is always having to look behind him, because he doesn't have any friends, and it's probably true that every devil in the universe thinks he could do a better job in the war against God. Lucifer is a rebel and a liar who is surrounded by rebels and liars, and that must be difficult.

Name number five: **The God of This World.**

This name, taken from Second Corinthians 4:4, is very much like "The Prince of This World," but it connotes even more of an authority over this planet. Of course, Lucifer is not really a God, he just wants to be one. But until the kingdom of heaven is ushered in with the dawning of the millennium, Lucifer and his forces exercise a great deal of control here.

Number six: **An Angel of Light** (Second Corinthians 11:14).

Sometimes, there is just enough truth in Lucifer's lie to

Strong's Concordance #142

make the whole thing look real. He's the master at making what's wrong look right, and vice versa. As I said before, if he should reveal himself to us the way he really is there would be very little about him that we would find appealing. So he comes to us in sweetness and light saying, as he did to Adam and Eve, "Oh, look...I know what God said, but He doesn't really *mean* it. What He really means is...." And then he takes us down the road of deception and destruction. But if you know God, and are standing solidly upon His Word, you will not be taken in by the false light that Lucifer tries to bring your way.

If you know anything about the Mormon religion, you know that Joseph Smith, the founder of that church, claimed to have been visited by angels of light. They told him where he could find the tablets that were later "translated" into the Book of Mormon. If Joseph Smith had known about Lucifer's ability to transform himself into an angel of light, he probably never would have written the Book of Mormon, and millions of innocent people wouldn't have been led down the path of destruction by a false religion!

So beware! Even though he is really The Prince of Darkness, Lucifer can and often does transform himself into an Angel of Light.

Let's go on and take a quick look at some of his other names.

The Serpent, Second Corinthians 11:3. There is nothing sneakier or slipperier than a snake!

Our Adversary, in 1 Peter 5:8.

We have no common ground with Lucifer. He has been our enemy from the beginning and always will be. A few years ago, The Rolling Stones recorded a song called "Sympathy for the Devil." Well, don't go feeling sorry for Lucifer because he doesn't feel sorry for you, and he wouldn't think for a single second about destroying you.

He is your adversary. He hates you.

The next name expresses this, too, for in Revelation 12:10, he is referred to as: **The Accuser of The Brethren.**

He loves to point the finger with you and tell your heavenly Father what a terrible person you are, to bring up all the sins you've committed. You might think of him as an evil prosecuting attorney, who is pointing out all your crimes and demanding that God punish you for them. But you know what? If you have been washed in the Blood of Jesus, when God looks at you all He sees is the righteousness of His Son.

And so Lucifer is ranting and raving and accusing you of all sorts of crimes that are worthy of punishment by death, and God looks at you and says, "I don't know what in the world you're talking about, Lucifer. This person looks totally innocent to me."

Praise God for the righteousness that is ours through faith in Christ!

Go ahead and accuse, Lucifer.

Now another way Lucifer accuses is by spreading false rumors. He loves to do that, to get people whispering about one another behind their backs, to get them spreading and believing lies about one another. Friends, you must be very careful about what you listen to, and strive to give your brothers and sisters in Christ the benefit of the doubt. When you hear something terrible about someone, just remember that Lucifer *loves* to accuse the brethren.

In Matthew 4:3, we find Lucifer referred to as: **The Tempter.**

Of course he's the tempter. He tempted Adam and Eve to sin way back in the Garden of Eden, and he's been tempting as many people as possible ever since then. Now just because you're being tempted, that does not mean that you are guilty of anything. We are all tempted, and the Bible is very clear that Jesus Himself was tempted by every temptation known to man. (Hebrews 4:15)

You're only guilty of sin when you give in to temptation and do the thing Lucifer is trying to get you to do.

But don't relax just because you've been able to deflect temptation the first time it comes. Lucifer doesn't give up, and he'll keep coming back and keep coming back and tempting you over and over again if you let him.

Sometimes, the temptation grows stronger and becomes harder to resist as time goes by.

Adultery, for example, is like that.

It may start out with simply thinking that some woman (or man) is nice, or sweet or good-looking. Then you're tempted to flirt a little bit, but you think it's okay, because that won't really hurt anyone. How about if you ask her out for an "innocent" lunch? And so step by step you're getting deeper and deeper into the temptation, until pretty soon you're deep into a full-blown affair and wondering how in the world you got here.

In John 10:10, Lucifer is referred to as **The Thief** that comes to steal, kill and destroy. And he is a thief. He will steal your money, your health, your joy, your family relationships, your position in the kingdom of God, your vision and passion for God's work, and he'd steal your very salvation if he could.

Lucifer loves to steal and he loves to get other people to steal, too. You know, some people have a sickness where they "can't help" but steal things. It doesn't really matter what it is. It may be something they don't have the slightest use for — but they see it, and they just *have* to have it. Those people are called "kleptomaniacs," but they are really controlled by an evil spirit that likes to steal. There is an inward agitation to these people that makes them feel like they just have to steal...and they need for someone to take authority over that demon of thievery in the name of Jesus and cast it out of them.

In John 8:44, Lucifer is called **The Murderer.**

And that he is. He has, in fact, killed every human being who has ever lived on this planet. What do I mean? Well, if it wasn't for Lucifer's temptation of Adam and Eve in the Garden of Eden, there wouldn't be any such thing as death. We would all live forever, joyously in the presence of God. And so Lucifer is a murderer in that way.

He is also a murderer in a more specific sense. He wants men and women to hate each other and kill each other. He delights in the teen gangs that engage in drive-by shootings, who think nothing of killing someone just because he's not wearing the right color clothes. Lucifer also takes great, great joy in the millions of abortions that are performed in this world each year. Lucifer loves to murder children because it destroys the next generation of leaders and revivalists. He killed the children when Moses was born, and he did it again when Christ was born. It's so sad that probably some of our greatest preachers have been murdered before they've ever been able to breath the natural air of this earth! And that's because Lucifer is a murderer!

He is also a murderer in that he loves to destroy the souls of men. He will take as many as possible with him into his place of torment. He wants to destroy *your* soul.

There are also specific murdering demons who seek to kill and injure.

Have you ever read a news story about a murder and seen the killer quoted as saying, "I just wanted to kill someone," or "I just wanted to see what it felt like to kill someone." Whenever someone says something like that, you can be fairly positive he has come under the influence of a murdering demon.

I have heard demons say, "I'm a demon who loves the taste and the smell of blood. I love to spill blood." This is a murdering spirit, and I have especially had to deal with them when I've been in foreign countries — Africa and Europe, some of these places where there have been so many civil wars and rebellions. What happens is that some of these soldiers get so used to murder and the spilling of human blood that they open themselves up to demonic influence. Due to their bondage to demon spirits, some of these soldiers actually become addicted to killing.

Do you remember the horror that Uganda went through under a man named Idi Amin? I was in that country shortly after he was driven from power, and I went down into the dungeon underneath the capitol building there in Kampala, and there were still blood stains on the walls. You may remember how Amin and his soldiers would torture and kill those they considered to be their enemies, and then practice cannibalism. I mean, they would actually butcher those people like they were cattle, take the meat home and eat it. How can we explain such horrible, horrible behavior? We can only explain it by pointing to the murdering nature of Lucifer and his demon armies.

When we are dealing with demons we are dealing with vicious, horrendous fiends. Yet we have nothing to fear so long as we are walking in the power of Christ.

One final name for Lucifer is found in First Peter 5:8, where he is described as **A Roaring Lion.**

Now there are only two places most of us ever see lions. The first place is the zoo and the second is the circus. And they're not that scary as long as they're kept behind iron bars in their cages. But I certainly wouldn't want to meet one out in the wild somewhere. Every once in awhile I'll see a newspaper story about a man-eating lion that's attacked a village in Africa and killed several villagers.

Lions, as you know, are huge cats. Have you ever watched a cat stalking its prey? It will crouch down and wait silently, almost without breathing, twitching its tail ever so slightly and just looking for the right moment to strike. And then, all of a sudden, it leaps into action, and it's on top of its prey before the poor victim has a chance to even think about escaping.

Well that's a very good description of Lucifer. He waits, and he watches, and he looks for the exact moment when the time is right to strike. There may be that one moment of weakness, that split second of carelessness. He's crouched, he's waiting, he's looking for someone to devour.

So be on alert!

We haven't discussed all of Lucifer's names. There are several more. But the ones we have mentioned here give you a pretty accurate understanding of his personality and his plan.

THE TALENTS OF DEMONS

Now, of course, the individual demons themselves have differing personalities, but they all have a particular area of wickedness — a certain "specialty" with which they seek to inflict human beings. For instance, a moment ago I talked about the existence of "murdering spirits." There are many other specific types of demons. Let's take a look at just a few of these.

First of all, the Bible has many warnings against "familiar spirits." For example, see Leviticus 19:31, 20:6, Deuteronomy 18:11, First Samuel 28:3. A familiar spirit is a demon that gets involved in seances, fortune-telling and such. Very often it will imitate the personalities of dead human beings. If you know anything about spirit mediums, seances and the like, you know that a spirit medium almost always has a "spirit guide." What happens is that the medium goes into a trance and the spirit guide takes over and controls the rest of the seance. Usually this spirit guide will pretend to be an ancient, wise and benevolent being. Well, it may be ancient, but it is not wise or benevolent. It is a demon, and what the Bible refers to as a "familiar spirit."

Matthew 12:22 mentions a blind spirit — which is a

demon that can cause physical *and* spiritual blindness. I have seen the eyes of blind people opened by the casting out of this spirit. It is a truly amazing thing when someone suddenly has vision, perhaps for the first time in his life. All of the colors, the lights, the visual sensations sink into that person's brain, and it really is like seeing someone being born.

First Kings 22:22-23 talks about "a lying spirit" which is simply a demon that makes people lie. You can give this particular demon entrance into your life just by telling a few lies...and that brings me to a special warning for parents. Folks, we've got to teach our children to tell the truth. If we don't teach them that honesty and truthfulness is important they will become liars, and a lying spirit will get hold of them. What happens is that a child will lie to avoid getting into trouble about something he's done. And if he gets away with it he'll start thinking that a lie can be better than the truth, and that opens the door wide for a lying spirit to walk through.

Sometimes what will happen is that a lying spirit or other demon will get into a young child's life, but stay pretty much hidden until that child grows up. Then it will manifest itself and cause all kinds of problems for that person and his friends and family. So, parents, for your children's sake, please watch carefully over them in this area.

First Timothy 4:1 refers to "a seducing spirit." This is a demon that will tempt you into sin and rejection of God's truth. This spirit may try to seduce you into immoral sexual activity. But it is just as likely to try to seduce you into "intellectualism," and rejection of God's truths because you've become "too smart to believe all that." You must always be on your guard against such spirits.

Matthew 18:18 talks about "a binding spirit." Have you ever felt that you were bound — like something had a hold of you and just wouldn't let you go. You want to have more faith in God but something is holding you back. You want to be happy but you're just so sad. You very well could be in the grip of a binding spirit, but the power of Christ can set you free.

Another type of demon is a foul spirit, which is mentioned in Mark 9:25 and Revelation 1:22. That is not a misnomer. There are demons that actually smell...have a terrible stench, in fact. Sometimes you can smell them when you're casting them out, and I have had occasions where I actually got sick to my stomach. It's not so much through the nose that you can smell them, but it's as if their stench almost overpowers your spirit.

Although there are many, many more specific types of demons, we're going to look at just two more.

The first is "a jealous spirit," which is described in Numbers 5:14. You've probably heard jealousy described as a "green-eyed monster." That's not far from the truth. Jealousy is a beast that can kill relationships, churches, organizations and people's lives. I have seen men of God virtually destroyed because someone became jealous of them. Jealousy is totally opposed to the spirit of Christ, and if you give in to this type of demon it can suck the life and joy right out of you.

The last type of spirit I want to talk about is "a religious spirit."

Now some people think that demons are afraid of a "Christian" church. They won't go near it simply because it has a cross on the roof and Bibles in the pews. Let me assure you that that is very far from the truth. It's possible for demons to feel right at home in many of America's churches today. Some churches have gone so far that they've even forgotten why it is we get together on Sunday morning. They're into this cause and that cause, even supplying guns and ammunition to terrorist groups around the world. They've forgotten the simple truth that Jesus Christ died, was buried and rose again on the third day, and that through His sacrifice we can obtain forgiveness of our sins. They have what the Bible calls "a form" of godliness, but they don't know a thing about God's power. (See Second Timothy 3:5)

Jesus told us that we are supposed to be the salt of the earth. Then He said that if salt has lost its saltiness it is good for nothing, so you might as well throw it out and walk on it. That's exactly what has happened in many of these churches. They've completely lost their saltiness and so they've become easy prey for the religious spirit.

I am sad to say it, but the truth is that when Christ comes, He will tell these so-called Christians that they have never really known Him, that they are "worthless" and He will cast them out.

As I said, these are only a few of the many types of demons that are at work in the world. But remember that it's not really necessary to know what sort of demon you're dealing with in order to cast it out. All demons are subject to the power and authority of Christ — and all must submit to the authority Christ gives to you as a born-again, spirit-filled Christian.

The plain fact is that if you belong to Christ, Lucifer and all of his demons are afraid of you. They hate you. They'd like to destroy you. But they know beyond any doubt that you're more powerful than they are.

The Bible puts it this way: *"More powerful is He who is in you than he who is in the world."* (1 John 4:4)

So go forward in the power and might of Christ, and conquer!

3

A HABITATION OF DEMONS

You can find the story in the fifth chapter of the Book of Mark.

Jesus and His disciples had come across the Sea of Galilee, into the country of the Gadarenes. No sooner had they arrived than they were met by a demon-possessed man — a man who had so many demons in him that they described themselves as being "legion."

This fellow was really something. Mark writes that he lived among the tombs — probably because the demons that had taken control of him were more comfortable around death and decay than they would have been anywhere else. Apparently, the people who lived nearby wanted desperately to get rid of this man. Several times they had attempted to capture him, wrapping him up with ropes and chains, but the demons made him so strong that he was able to break the chains and escape.

Mark goes on to say that this man was always cutting himself with stones and crying out. In other words, he was so much under the influence of demons that he had no control at all over his own actions.

It's interesting to see, though, that as soon as Jesus got off the boat, this fellow ran and fell on his knees in front of Him and worshipped Him. The demons within him recognized Jesus immediately, knew that He was the Lord, and they weren't going to try to defy him even for a moment. Instead, they caused their human host to fall down in front of the Lord, and they begged Jesus not to torment them before their time for judgment had come.

The demons that were in-dwelling this man knew immediately that Jesus was going to cast them out. They knew that one of the missions of Jesus was to "set the captives free," and so they didn't even try to beg Him not to drive them out of the man. Instead, they began looking frantically for an alternative — somewhere else they could live.

Looking around, they spied a huge herd of pigs. Well, any port in a storm, you know, and so they asked the Lord if He wouldn't please, please let them go into the pigs.

The Bible says that Jesus gave them permission — which, once again, shows that He has complete authority over demon power. But something very unusual happened when they went into those pigs. Those animals were so terrorized that they ran right down the hill, and on out into the sea, where they all drowned.

You can imagine how terrified the pig-farmer must have been. All of a sudden, his pigs are going absolutely crazy. He's running around trying to get them under control, but he just can't do it. They're snorting and oinking and carrying on like a bunch of demon-possessed pigs, which is exactly what they were. It must have been an amazing sight to see!

The Bible says there were 2,000 pigs in this herd, and every one of them rushed into the sea and was drowned. Can you imagine the story that pig-farmer told the next time he was in town.

"Joseph, you're not going to believe this...but I was out with the pigs...you know, it was just an ordinary day...and all of a sudden they just went crazy. They were whirling around and snorting and bucking like broncos. And then they all ran right into the sea and drowned!"

"All of them?"

"Every one!"

Strong's Concordance #5228

"Is this an April Fools' joke?"

Well, I don't know why the pigs ran into the sea and were drowned, but it really happened. More than likely, what happened was the pigs simply reacted to the demons entering their bodies. They were frightened, they panicked, and they wound up destroying themselves.

It's interesting to me that these "dumb" animals were panicked by the sudden appearance of demons among them, but many human beings will open themselves totally to demon influences and never give it a second thought. We even have people who worship Satan, and who invite demons to enter into them; not only invite them, in fact, but beg them. Such total foolishness! You might as well put a sign in front of your house saying, "Thieves welcome! Come on in and steal us blind! Rob us! Kill us! Please!"

It just doesn't make sense.

WHERE DO THEY LIVE?

Now so far in this book we've talked about the fact that demons are responsible for haunted houses, ghostly sightings and such. And then we've spent some time taking a look at where demons come from. In this chapter, I want to take a look at where demons live. And that's why I've started off with the story of the legion of demons and the herd of swine.

This story tells us two things about where demons like to live. First, they like to live in human beings. Second, if humans aren't available to them, they will go into animals.

You see, a demon wants to have a fleshly body, partly because he enjoys the sins of the flesh so much. A demon wants to over-eat, drink to excess, take drugs, engage in all sorts of sexual perversions, and he needs a body to do these things. A human body is preferable, of course, but if he has trouble getting one of those he'll take whatever else might be available to him.

If even that fails, and no animal is susceptible to his influences, a demon will decide to occupy a certain territory — an old house, a stretch of woods, an isolated lake. Our ancestors knew instinctively about these things. There were certain places they wouldn't go near because they understood that they were under an evil influence. Modern man has, to a great extent, stopped believing in such things. He has gotten too "smart" for his own good, too "sophisticated" for his own safety.

Not too long ago, I came across a true story about five college students who decided that they were too smart and too sophisticated to believe in evil spirits or ghosts or anything of the sort. They went out to a certain location near their school that was supposedly "haunted," and they made fun of whatever spirits were present in that place. They ridiculed them, and challenged them, and dared them to make their presence known.

They thought it was all so much fun.

Unfortunately, though, these students did not belong to Jesus. They figured that those who believed in Him were just as foolish as those who believed in evil spirits. Because of their unbelief, they were not protected by the Blood of Christ, and the demons of that place apparently decided to take them up on their dare.

Within six months of their visit to the "haunted" area, all of those college students had dropped out of school. Friends who knew them said they had become paranoid and fearful. They talked about strange things happening to them — about hearing voices, and seeing disembodied spirits and feeling that their lives were in danger. Basically, those young men went into hiding. Goals and dreams were abandoned. They had learned a very important lesson about the reality of the supernatural world, but they had learned it at a very great cost.

Now I don't want to give you the impression that every

so-called "haunted house" is actually the home of a demon (or demons). Most "haunted houses" are nothing more than old buildings that have become a little run-down and creepy looking, and because they look sort of "scary," people let their imaginations run away with them. There is far too much paranoia in the world, and I don't want to feed it. But it is vitally important to understand that some haunted houses really are haunted.

Almost always, in a case like this, you'll find out that the demon was attracted to the place by some tragedy that happened there. Demons especially seem to be drawn by the spilling of human blood.

And then, there are places that have been dedicated to Satan, and which are full of demons because of that.

I know of one instance, as a matter of fact, where an entire *country* was dedicated to Satan — and that is the tiny island nation of Haiti. Now Haiti is the poorest country in the Western Hemisphere, if not in the entire world. It is an incredibly impoverished, backwards country, and it's a country that is very much into demonism.

Haiti has been through a series of repressive governments. It's a place where you can still hear Voodoo drums at night, and where, legend has it, zombies sometimes roam the countryside at night. Well, you know, I don't believe in zombies, but I sure do believe in the existence of demons.

Part of the reason for Haiti's trouble is that more than 200 years ago, one of the governors of Haiti was a Satanist. He had an official ceremony in which he dedicated the country to the devil, and effectively "handed over" Haiti to Lucifer's control. Poor Haiti has had terrible trouble ever since.

Now, I am not saying that there are not good Christian people in Haiti. But there are many more who have Christianity all bound up with Voodooism, and so there is an intense battle between the forces of good and evil in that country.

So to recap, we can see three places where demons like to live:

1) Human beings.

2) Animals.

3) Places.

There are also some other, more specific areas where demons like to congregate.

For example, demons love to be around the seat of political power.

Before I say anything further let me tell you that I am proud to be an American. I love this country, and I thank God for the freedoms we enjoy here. Furthermore, I think Washington D.C. is a beautiful and impressive city, with all those marble monuments, the White House, the Capitol Building, and so on. But we're missing something important if we get dazzled by all that history and beauty and power and don't realize that the city of Washington has demonic activity.

QUEST FOR POWER

Demons love power. They've always loved hanging around kings and emperors and presidents and congressmen and so on. That's not to say that there haven't been many fine men and women who have dedicated themselves to government service. But Christians who go into politics have a struggle in front of them, because they are going to be surrounded by demonic influence.

If you go back through history and read about the powerful kings and queens of old, you might be amazed at how many of them seemed to be absolutely crazy. Some were terribly cruel...like Herod who ordered all the little babies murdered, or Nero, who murdered most of his own family, and who used human beings as torches to light his gardens. There have been so many bloodthirsty tyrants from biblical times right up until today. Why? Because wherever you find political power, you will also find demons.

If you need more proof that political power and demons go together, just take a moment to think about the laws that are coming out of Washington these days: Laws to restrict religious freedom, laws to make abortion easier and more readily available, laws to curtail the rights of parents, laws to make it easier for criminals to get away with their crimes. Yes, indeed, Washington has demonic influences.

Not too long ago, I read about a case where the court took a young man away from his parents and placed him in a foster home. Why? Because his parents were "forcing him" to go to Wednesday night Bible study at their church. The boy, who was 14, went to his junior high school counselor and complained about it. The counselor, who was apparently an atheist, was aghast, and turned the parents in to government authorities.

The reason was that the boy was growing up in an "unhealthy" environment. The last I heard, the case was going to court in the state of Washington. Hopefully, a ruling will be made in favor of the parents. But they never should have had to go through all of this turmoil, pain and expense in the first place.

You can bet there are hundreds of demons laughing about this one!

Again, I guarantee you, you will find demons in the world of politics. You will also find them living very close to the centers of financial power.

You will find very strong demonic power around those who control money. Money has a way of taking over people's hearts and minds so that they are unable to give themselves to God. Some rich people start thinking that they don't need God...and when you've swept Him out of your life, then you're opening yourself to influences from the other side.

Have you ever noticed that some people who have a lot of money can't seem to get enough of it. They may amass such a huge pile of money that they couldn't possibly spend it all in a dozen lifetimes, and yet they keep striving for more, more, more! No wonder the Bible says that the love of money is the root of all kinds of evil. (First Timothy 6:10)

PRINCIPALITIES

Another thing you need to understand about demons is that there are certain types who have control over particular cities or areas (called 'principality', Eph. 6:12).

For example, have you ever wondered why there is so much homosexual activity within the city of San Francisco? It's true, you know. In fact, if you're a tourist in San Francisco, they'll give you a map that highlights different areas of the city, and that map will guide you right to the homosexual neighborhoods. They are actually *proud* of the sexual perversion that takes place in their city, and try to use it as a tourist attraction! Amazing!

But you see, the principality who is in charge of San Francisco is a demon of homosexuality, and so you are going to find all sorts of like-minded demons there, along with all sorts of sexual perversions.

If you'll take your Bible and turn to the sixth chapter of Ephesians, verse twelve, you'll find Paul's warning that we are not battling against flesh and blood, but against, as the King James Version says, "principalities and powers" of darkness.

So there are divisions and duties within the demonic realm, and there are powerful demons that have control over specific cities and areas.

If you get to the point where you are sensitive to such things, to where God gives you a great degree of discernment, you can begin to feel the demonic powers that exist within a certain city or area.

For example, I could never live in New York City because there is a spirit of violence there. The city is strongly influenced by demons of violence and murder and fear, and I would just not want to live in a place where I felt those things so strongly. No, I wouldn't be afraid because I have the Spirit of Christ within me, but I would be depressed to be surrounded by such evil, and it would be very difficult for me. In the same way, I would not want to live in San Francisco because of that controlling spirit of homosexuality and perversion.

Now if you happen to live in New York or San Francisco, please don't be offended with me. I'm not equating your city with Sodom or Gomorrah. Every city has its controlling demon. That doesn't mean the city is entirely sold out to Lucifer, but it means that Lucifer has appointed one of his powerful generals to be in charge of demon activity within the city — to engage in spiritual warfare against the people who live there.

Now some people are attracted to certain cities because of the demonic activity that takes place in them. For instance, homosexuals have come from all over to settle in San Francisco because they know they'll be free in that city to indulge in their favorite sin without fear of being exposed. In the same way, a criminal might be attracted to New York because there is so much violence there already he feels that he has a pretty good chance of getting away with whatever criminal activity he wants to pursue.

If you live in an area, you've got to know the controlling demons so you can stand against them — so you can pray and strengthen yourself and be on guard against the particular demons that are trying to destroy all the people who live in your city.

There are people who think nothing of going to church on Sunday morning and evening but drinking and carousing and doing whatever else they want to do during the week. You've heard the old saying — pray like a saint on Sunday morning and live like the devil the rest of the week.

Another place I lived was in the northern U.S. and there was a Jezebel spirit there, a spirit of rebellion that destroyed some men who could have been great leaders in the kingdom of God.

There were some men there who had powerful churches and large followings. But when other men began to teach about the importance of faith, they didn't understand it, so they spoke out against it. They spoke out against it with great vehemence and passion. They didn't even wait to see if God was involved in what was being said, but immediately went on the attack.

What those men were doing was that they were getting right into step with the controlling demon of their city. As a result, they opened themselves up to other demonic influences. Some of them got involved in adultery, and alcoholism, and all sorts of things — and some of them are wandering the streets of Minneapolis today, drunken, helpless bums! It's pathetic, but it's a prime example of what demons can do to a man or woman.

You have to know where demons live, and know the ways in which they will try to attack you. There is a battle going on out there...and you're in it whether you realize it or not.

Never think you're exempt. Always keep a watch on yourself. Keep in constant prayer. Check your thoughts and actions against the Word of God. Don't be fooled into thinking something is okay because everyone else does it.

I was preaching in Las Vegas a few months ago, and I was reminded of a story Lester Sumrall tells about one of his experiences there. He was called to preach at a particular church, and after his sermon, when the time came to give him the offering, the treasurer of that church asked him if he wanted his honorarium in money or casino chips.

When Brother Sumrall expressed surprise over the question and said that, of course, he didn't want the casino chips, the treasurer told him that his experience was that most visiting preachers took the chips. Can you imagine? They'd come in and preach about the importance of living a godly life, and then they'd be paid in chips so they could go down and spend their evenings playing roulette and black jack and what-have-you.

You see, even men and women of God have been seduced. They believe it's okay to gamble and see X-rated movies and do anything at all they want to do just because "everybody else is doing it." It is so easy to slide into demonic activity before you know what's happened to you.

Let's recap what we've learned in this chapter about where demons like to live.

1) The first choice of any demon would be to possess a human body — primarily because it gives him a chance to indulge himself in the sins of the flesh.

2) If a human body isn't available, a demon may choose to enter into an animal — whether it's a pig, a cat, a dog, or any other kind of creature.

3) If a demon is not able to enter into a living creature, it may take up residence in a particular place: A house, a patch of woods, a lake, etc.

4) Many demons will be found in close proximity to centers of political power — including Washington, D.C.

5) Demons also love to involve themselves in the world of high finance and commerce. As we've seen, money really is the root of all kinds of evil.

6) Every city has a particular controlling demon (and demons), and for that reason different cities are noted for different types of sinful behavior.

Again, I want to remind you that it's important not to give demons too much credit, and not to let ourselves spend too much time thinking about them. But at the same time, it's important to know as much about demons as we possibly can — how they operate, where they like to live, where they come from, etc. That's because the more we understand about demons, the more we will be able to take action against them — the more we will be able to defeat them.

Now, how should you act when you are confronted by demonic power? You should act the same way Jesus Christ acted when He came into contact with demons.

We're going to take a look at Jesus' interaction with demons in Chapter Four.

4

FOLLOWING JESUS INTO BATTLE

Some people seem to think that the more spiritual you are, the less you'll have to do with demons. Well, to quote the old song, "it ain't necessarily so."

In fact, just the opposite is likely to be true. It is usually true that the more you strive to follow Christ, to be like Him, and to reflect His glory, the *more* encounters you'll have with these creatures from hell.

Christ is our example and our pattern, and if we get to the point where we truly reflect him, then we're going to have more, not less, contact with demons for two reasons. First, because the demons will seek us out in an attempt to get us to stop living for Jesus. They don't like Christians, because Christians are going about the business of snatching human souls out of their grip. The demons want to stop you because, as a spirit-filled born-again Christian, you are a real threat to them.

The second reason a Christian is likely to have more open confrontations with demons is because God is likely to lead you into situations where confrontation is necessary. It is His power within you that assures your victory over the forces of hell, and He wants you to use that power to advance His kingdom, *and* to set free the captives of Lucifer and his armies.

Of course, when it comes to preparation for dealing with demons, nothing could serve us better than studying the life of Christ. Our Savior had many battles with devils throughout His earthly lifetime, beginning very early in His ministry.

THE GREAT TEMPTATION

In fact, if you'll turn over to the fourth chapter of Matthew, you'll find out that the first thing Jesus did, upon the official beginning of His ministry was that He went into the wilderness to be tempted by Satan (or Lucifer).

Now why do I say that this was "the official beginning" of His ministry? Because for the first 30 years of His life, Jesus apparently stayed pretty much in the background. (As much, at least, as was possible for the Son of God. Remember, of course that there was that one incident when he was 12 years old and he confounded the scribes and Pharisees at the temple with His wisdom.) But at the age of 30, He came to His cousin John the Baptist and asked to be baptized.

This was a significant event, because it was at this time that Jesus received a special anointing of the Holy Spirit and God's voice from heaven spoke, declaring, *"This is my beloved Son."* (Matthew 3:16-17) It was at this particular time that the focus shifted from John to Jesus. The time had come, as John put it, that Jesus was to increase in power and influence, and he was to decrease. (John 3:30)

Immediately after His baptism, Jesus went into the wilderness, where He was tempted by the devil.

During this time, we read that Jesus fasted for forty days and nights. Now before we continue, I need to give you a bit of advice, and that is that you should never ever go on a fast of this length unless God specifically commands it, and even then you had better be sure you're really listening to God. A prolonged fast can do tremendous damage to the mind, body and spirit. I've known people who've undergone such a fast, but instead of coming back with power and anointing they've wound up with goofy ideas and weakness of mind. I don't want to be harsh, but I'm telling the truth, and I think a word of warning is necessary.

Jesus knew what He was doing...no doubt about it. And part of what He was doing was preparing for the ordeal of the next three years, up to and including His death on the cross.

Naturally, when His fast was over, Jesus was hungry. That's probably one of the great understatements of all time. He was *more* than hungry. He was famished!

And so Lucifer came to him saying, in essence, "You poor fellow. I know you must be starved half to death. But, listen...if you're *really* the Son of God, why don't you just turn some of these stones into bread?" Can't you just see the concerned look on Lucifer's face. He looks *so* compassionate.

But Christ withstood that temptation. Looking his adversary square in the eyes, the Lord replied, *"It is written: Man does not live on bread alone, but on every word that comes from the mouth of God."* (Matthew 4:4)

THE TOOLS OF BATTLE

And there's lesson number one for being a successful devil-fighter. Hit them right in the face with the Scriptures. Give them chapter and verse from the Word of God. That's something they can't withstand, and it's something they can't fight.

Of course, in order to hit them with the Word of God, you've got to *know* the Word of God. And in order to know the Word of God, you've got to spend time with it — not only reading it, but meditating on it, digesting it, memorizing it. If you know what God has to say about things, then there's no way Lucifer or one of his henchmen can trick you.

In Jesus' case, Lucifer didn't even try to argue with Him. He was blasted by the Scripture, and there was nothing he could do but turn his attention elsewhere.

In this instance, he took Christ up to the top of the temple and tried to get Him to jump off. He was like a child, saying, "Come on, prove it to me. You're supposed to be the Son of God, but I really find that hard to believe. However, if you'll prove it by jumping off the temple and letting your angels carry you safely to the ground below...well, then I'll really be convinced."

This time, Lucifer himself attempted to use Scripture.

"For it is written," he said, "'He will command his angels concerning you, and they will lift you up in their hands, so that you will not strike your foot against a stone.'"

Matthew 4:6

Don't think for a moment that demons don't know the Bible. They know it very well. I'm ashamed to say it, but they know it better than some of those who consider themselves to be Christians. Lucifer and his followers seem to love nothing more than to twist the Scriptures and try to convince people that the Word of God says something it doesn't really say at all. And, once again, the only way to combat that is to know the Bible for yourself. If you do, you won't be fooled when Lucifer tries to take an isolated verse out of context and twist it all out of shape.

Right now, for instance, there is a controversial religious group called The Family. They used to be known as The Children of God, and they consider themselves to be Christian. But they have totally twisted Christ's words about love. Somewhere along the line, these people began to confuse sex with love. They even went so far as to teach their followers that they should attempt to use sex to bring others into God's kingdom. They taught their young girls to use their bodies as a means of evangelism. Can you imagine anything so perverse, so far away from the true teachings of Scripture? And yet that is the sort of thing that can happen when people listen to Lucifer's twisting of the Word of God.

Anyway, in this instance, Lucifer was trying to get Jesus to use His power not for some great purpose, but merely to show off, and of course, our Lord wouldn't have anything at all to do with it. Once again, Christ deflected Satan with a word from the Bible — a word quoted correctly: *"It is also written: 'Do not put the Lord your God to the test.'"* (Matthew 4:7)

Once again, Lucifer was defeated. But that didn't mean he was through trying.

This time, the Bible says, he took Christ up to a very high mountain and showed him "all the kingdoms" of the world. Then he told the Lord he would surrender all of these kingdoms to Him, if only He would bow down and worship Lucifer.

Think about what a temptation that must have been. Jesus had come to redeem the world through His death on the cross. He could look into the future and see a time when He was going to be rejected by His friends, beaten savagely by Roman soldiers, and then nailed to a cross and killed. And Lucifer was saying, in essence, "Hey, you don't have to go through all of that. Just bow down and worship me, and I'll *give* you all these things. You don't have to go through any of that agony!"

Of course, Christ knew that if He bowed down to Lucifer, even for an instant, the war would be over, and Lucifer would have won. He would have brought Almighty God to his knees — which had been his objective all along.

And then, Christ also knew that those kingdoms were not the devil's to give.

Do you ever look around and get to wondering why people who seem to live such wicked lives do so well in this world? Some of them seem to be blessed. They have beautiful homes, drive fancy cars, and have more money in the bank than they know what to do with. From all appearances it looks like selling out to Satan has paid off.

Someone who didn't know any better might think, "If that's how Satan treats his people, then I'm all for him."

But, you see, all of those things are only temporary. They will not last, and when they come crashing down, the fall thereof will be mighty indeed. Furthermore, there will be a terrible, terrible price to pay. Jesus would not bow before Lucifer, and neither should you.

After trying so hard to get Jesus to abort His mission, and failing every time, Lucifer gave up. The Bible says that the devil left Jesus, and that angels then came and ministered to the Lord. (Matthew 4:11)

But when Lucifer retreats, it's never for good. He only retreats far enough and long enough to plan the next series of attacks in his battle for the human soul. That's a lesson for all of us. Don't ever think that you can let your guard down. The moment you do, he'll be waiting, like that "roaring lion" we talked about in the last chapter, and he'll pounce. We always have to be ready, always on our guard.

And so Jesus knew that he hadn't seen the last of the devil or his foot-soldiers.

To read about His next encounter with demons, turn over to the ninth chapter of Matthew.

In the 32nd verse of that chapter, we find the story of a man who was possessed by a demon that kept him from speaking. As soon as Jesus cast the demon out of him, the man began to speak.

I have had some encounters with this type of demon. Sometimes, the person with such a devil cannot speak at all, and other times he is kept from speaking at particular times. For example, I have seen occasions when demon-possessed people got into a prayer line, but then couldn't tell me what they wanted or needed.

I would ask what the problem was, and they would just stand there staring at me. I could look into the eyes and see that the wheels were turning. This person *wanted* to say something, but just couldn't.

If you're tuned in, it's fairly easy to see, in this situation, that a demon is involved, and once you've cast out the demon in the name of Jesus, the problem is solved.

Now if you skip down to verse 34, you'll find that the Pharisees had a typical reaction to what Jesus was doing. They said he was able to cast out devils only because He was in league with the prince of demons.

ACCUSATIONS

Well, you know, people haven't really changed very much over the last 2,000 years. When God first began to reveal to me that He wanted me to be involved in the business of setting people free from demons, a lot of people didn't like it. They were embarrassed by it, because the process of casting demons out can be noisy, and messy, and disturbing. They wanted me to have nice, quiet church services where nothing much happened. But what could I do? There were so many people in bondage, and I wasn't going to walk away from them. Besides, the Lord said, "Do it," and so I really didn't have any choice in the matter anyway.

Some people were so upset by what I was doing that they said the same thing the Pharisees had said about Jesus — that I myself was possessed by demons.

My answer was, "All right, if I've got demons, help me get rid of them. Cast them out of me."

I didn't have any takers.

Turning over to the twelfth chapter of Matthew, we find Christ experiencing another encounter with demons and Pharisees. This time a demon-possessed man who was both blind and mute was brought to Christ, and, once again, He cast out the demon and the man was healed of his infirmities. The ordinary people were so impressed that they began to wonder out loud if Jesus might not be the Messiah they had waited for so long. But not the Pharisees. Once more, their astute conclusion was that Jesus was in league with Beelzebub (another name for Lucifer).

It was at this point that our Lord reminded the Pharisees that "a house divided against itself cannot stand." If Lucifer himself was going around casting demons out of people, then we could just sit back and watch his evil kingdom fall apart.

Are people being benefitted by a ministry of deliverance? Absolutely. Lives are being changed dramatically. Alcoholics and drug addicts are being instantly set free as demons are driven out. People are finding deliverance from all sorts of things that have plagued them for years. Lucifer never does anything to help anyone...so it is totally preposterous to think that he is responsible for the casting out of demons.

My point, though, is that if you are prepared to fight demons, you should also be prepared to deal with the slanderous accusations that some people are going to toss at you. There are going to be people who won't understand, and who will accuse you of all sorts of things. I guarantee it.

ANOINTING

Part of the reason for that is that the anointing of deliverance is a stronger, rougher, more militant anointing than the anointing for healing. It is an anointing that will put you immediately into combat situations. Make no mistake about it — deliverance is war. Some people would like to pretend that we're not at war — but we are!

I have been in crusades where I have prayed for people who have been in demonic bondage for 10 or 15 years, and when I do they began to shake and jerk uncontrollably. Their regular pastor is looking on and thinking, "Well, I've prayed for you before. Why didn't you jump like that when

I prayed." Well, that pastor didn't ask God to give him a deliverance anointing. Perhaps he even sought not to receive such an anointing because he didn't want to look foolish. If you want to see people set free, you can't worry about things like your appearance!

Jesus didn't worry about His dignity, and He was the Son of God. If He had worried about such things, He never would have allowed Himself to be born in a manger. He never would have associated with the likes of prostitutes and tax collectors. But He got right down there in the dirt, so to speak, because He knew that's where the hurting people were, the ones who *knew* they needed His help.

As we read through the Book of Matthew, we find that our Lord's next encounter with demons is recorded in the 15th chapter:

"A Canaanite woman from that vicinity came to him, crying out, 'Lord, Son of David, have mercy on me! My daughter is suffering terribly from demon-possession.'

"Jesus did not answer a word, So his disciples came to him and urged him, 'Send her away, for she keeps crying out after us.'

"He answered, 'I was sent only to the lost sheep of Israel.'

"The woman came and knelt before him. 'Lord, help me!' she said.

"He replied, 'It is not right to take the children's bread and toss it to their dogs.'

"'Yes, Lord,' she said, 'but even the dogs eat the crumbs that fall from their masters' table.'

"Then Jesus answered, 'Woman, you have great faith! Your request is granted.' And her daughter was healed from that very hour."

Matthew 15:22-28, NIV

AUTHORITY

The Scriptures don't tell us how old this woman's daughter was, but based on my own experience I wouldn't be surprised if she was no more than seven or eight years old, and perhaps even younger. You see, parents are responsible for bringing deliverance and help to their children. If you don't keep authority over your children and teach them how to live for the Lord while they're growing up, devils will come in and live with them. That's why we read stories in our newspapers about twelve and thirteen-year-olds doing things like shooting their parents or their neighbors and never showing the least little bit of remorse.

Not too long ago, I happened to be at home one afternoon, flipped on the television, and caught a few minutes of one of the popular talk shows. On this particular show they were featuring children who had given their parents all kinds of grief. The parents were sitting up there with their children, talking about all of the terrible things they had been through.

Now some of the people in the studio audience were quick to blame the parents for their children's misbehavior, saying things like, "If you'd disciplined them once in awhile this wouldn't have happened."

One of the mothers in particular became very angry over such allegations.

"You don't know how many times I corrected my child," she said. "How many times I punished him and spanked him, and did everything I could think of to change his behavior, and he still wouldn't change."

Well, I have no doubt at all that that lady was telling the truth. But you see, she didn't know anything about divine correction. But I also knew that some of the children being featured on that show did what they did because they had evil spirits living within them. It was just obvious. And an evil spirit cannot be hurt in any way by a spanking.

What goes on in a situation like that is that the demon causes the child to do something that's going to get him or her into trouble. Perhaps the child is completely out of control. Maybe he doesn't even remember afterwards what it was he did. But then when it comes time for the spanking to be administered, the spirit is somewhere laughing, and the child is left to suffer the pain. All that does is cause the child to suffer even further damage.

What the children on that talk show needed was someone to minister to them in the name of Jesus, someone to take authority over the evil spirits in those children and cast them out.

We read a lot these days about child abuse, and I think it's a terrible problem in our society. But much of the time, it is brought about by demons that get inside of children and then torture and torment the parents until they totally lose their tempers and end up battering what is really an innocent child. It is also true that child abuse is often caused by demons of rage, anger and bitterness that have taken up residence in the parents.

Again, I have to give a word of caution. I don't want to imply that all cases of child abuse come as the result of the work of evil spirits. Some people are just plain guilty of being mean and abusive to their children — but there are many, many instances when demons are involved.

Sometimes people ask me, "Do you really think a little child can be indwelt by an evil spirit?"

Yes ma'am, and yes sir, I do. I believe it because I've seen it with my own eyes.

And it can be an amazing thing to see.

Little boys come for prayer in their little suits, with their hair combed neatly, and looking like perfect little gentlemen. Little girls come with bows in their hair, wearing their pretty dresses and looking for all the world like little porcelain dolls.

But then when I lay hands on them, they'll begin to growl and moan and jerk as the demons fight to stay in them. Parents, your innocent, sweet children are not immune to demonic attack, and I'm not telling you that to scare you. I'm telling you because it's something you need to know.

I specifically remember one case in Minneapolis when a woman called and asked if she could bring in her daughter for prayer. She explained to me that the girl sometimes became violent and would beat her mother with her fists, throw things at her, and so on.

I figured we were probably talking about a teenager, and so I was surprised when that mother showed up with a little girl who couldn't have been more than 10 years old, and was probably younger than that. First of all, they came to a Sunday morning service when I was preaching, and I immediately knew who they were. The little girl was nervous and fidgety throughout the service, and it was not the normal type of energy one might associate with children. She was up and down, up and down, and left to go to the bathroom several times during the course of the service.

When her mother finally brought her to the altar for prayer, I laid hands on her and she immediately began to scream and kick. The ushers came running to help me, but they were too late! I had already received a vicious kick in the shin!

Well, once we had control of the situation, I was able to take authority over the demons in that little girl, and cast them out of her by the power and the name of Jesus. And when she left the church that morning she was smiling and happy, and acting like the sweetest little girl you ever saw. The difference was amazing. She had come down to the altar that morning acting for all the world like some wicked witch, and she had left acting like Rebecca of Sunnybrook Farm! That's what the Lord had done for her.

If you want to be involved in a ministry of deliverance, you will undoubtedly come across situations such as the one I've just described. Never, ever let a child go away from you still in bondage. But at the same time, parents have to keep divine authority over their children so that the demons do not come back once they have been driven out.

Another thing we learn from this story about the Canaanite woman is that deliverance is part of the "children's bread." It's a basic part of the Gospel. I've heard people say, "I'm not into deliverance." Well, if you're not into deliverance, then you're not into the basics of the gospel. Dealing with demons, bringing deliverance to the captives, should be one of the primary tenets of the Christian faith. Everyone in your church should be taught how to cast out devils, from your teenagers on to your oldest members.

CONTROL THROUGH CHRIST

Now I want to move on to just two more incidents from the life of Christ. The first is found in the first chapter of the Book of Mark. Jesus was in the village of Capernaum on the Sabbath day, and so He went to the synagogue and began to teach. The scriptures tell us that the people were astonished because He was talking to them as though He had authority. In other words, He made the Scriptures come alive to them. He knew what He was talking about and they could tell.

It happened that there was a man sitting among the worshipers at that synagogue who was afflicted with an evil spirit. Suddenly, right in the middle of things he cried out, "What do you want with us, Jesus of Nazareth? Have you come to destroy us? I know who you are — the Holy One of God!"

Now picture this scene if you will, because this is the way it would happen today. This man is sitting there in church, with his arm draped around his pretty wife, and his two adorable kids, a boy and a girl, sitting next to him. And all of a sudden, he begins to scream out, "Leave us alone, Jesus! Leave us alone!" I mean, right in the middle of the sermon, he starts hollering like a stuck pig. It probably scared his wife, and most of the rest of the people in that synagogue, half to death.

Now what did Jesus do? Did he summon the ushers and tell them to escort the gentleman outside because he was disrupting the service? No, Jesus simply ordered the demon to come out of the man, and the Bible says that the demon obeyed, "crying out with a loud voice" as it did so. The New International Version says that demon came out of the man "with a shriek."

Jesus took authority over the situation, cast the demon out with a few simple words, and then went on with his sermon.

What I want you to see about this situation is that Jesus maintained control. He didn't let the demon put on a big show and distract everyone's attention from worshiping God. He dealt with things directly and as simply as possible, and that's the way we are to do it as we follow Him. Now there are times when demon-possessed people will yell, and kick, and struggle, and do all sorts of things, but we still must deal with them as quickly as we possibly can, especially if they are doing all of those things in the middle of the church service, and then get on with what we've come together for, which is to worship God and learn from His Word.

Another thing I want you to see is that demons will react to the presence of God. This demon was prompted to show itself by the authority of Christ, and as we are representatives of Christ, full of the Holy Spirit, demons may also begin to manifest themselves in our presence.

For example, I live in Southern California, not too far from a place that is crawling with demons of all types. I'm talking about Hollywood in general, and the Sunset Strip in particular. Any born-again, spirit-filled Christian who walks down the Sunset Strip after dark is going to see demons manifesting themselves. You'll see some people glaring at you for no reason, and others hurrying away from you. Some people might yell at you. They won't know why, but it's because they have demons in them, and those demons are reacting to the presence of the Spirit of God, and the authority of His Spirit.

One thing that made some people angry with me a few years ago was that they would come to my meetings, and the deliverance anointing would be so strong that demons would begin to manifest all over the room. Some people said I was working the people into a frenzy, or getting them to act like they were being delivered. But that wasn't it at all. What was happening was that the authority was there, and the demons couldn't stand it, and began to show themselves. Don't ever think for a moment that just because someone is sitting in church, he can't be demonized. That's just not true. I hate to say it, but sometimes the safest place for a demon to hide is in church. Too many churches don't believe in the ministry of deliverance. Some don't even believe in the existence of demons. And you can't set somebody free from something you don't believe in. What they're doing, really, is telling those who are troubled by demons, "I'm sorry, but I can't help you, because I don't think you really have a problem." What a tragedy!

If pastors throughout America would read up on deliverance, if they'd scour the Scriptures to find out everything it's possible to know about the casting out of demons, if they would ask God to give them the anointing for deliverance...well, one of the greatest revivals of all time would sweep through this nation, no doubt about it.

PREPARE TO WIN

I want to look at one more encounter between Christ and demons before we move on, and that is the one described in the ninth chapter of Mark.

What happened here was that Jesus was coming down from the mountain after His Transfiguration. Peter, James and John were with him. And when they got down to where the other nine Apostles were, they saw that they were surrounded by a large group of people, and that there was a big commotion going on.

When all those people saw Jesus coming, they all ran to Him, and one of the men explained what was going on. It seems he had brought his demon-possessed son to the Apostles, and asked them to drive the demon out of the boy, but they couldn't do it.

"'Teacher, I brought you my son, who is possessed by a spirit that has robbed him of speech. Whenever it seizes him, it throws him to the ground. He foams at the mouth, gnashes his teeth and becomes rigid. I asked your disciples to drive out the spirit, but they could not.'

"O unbelieving generation,' Jesus replied, 'how long shall I stay with you? How long shall I put up with you? Bring the boy to me.'"

Mark 9:17-19, NIV

Jesus asked the father how long his son had been troubled by this spirit, and the man explained that it had been this way since early childhood. Imagine the terror and the suffering this poor boy and his family, had been put through. The poor, beleaguered father tells Jesus that sometimes the spirit will throw his son into the water, or at other times into the fire. Notice the self-destructive rage of this demon — so violent that it engages in behavior that could severely injure, or even kill, its human host. There is no thought for anything except giving vent to its anger and its loathing for human life.

Verse 20 tells us, *"When the spirit saw Jesus, it immediately threw the boy into a convulsion. He fell to the ground and rolled around, foaming at the mouth."*

That's a pretty good depiction of the sort of manifestation you might expect when someone is in the control of an evil spirit. In fact, based on what I've seen, I'd say this is one of the best descriptions of demon-controlled behavior in all the Bible. This is just so typical of the sort of behavior you'll encounter when you're dealing with demons. It can be frightening at first, but God will give you the courage and the strength to keep on. Sometimes it's like my natural mind wants to run away from it all, but my spirit is so tuned in to God that it will just keep me in there until the job is finished and the demon has gone.

Let's move on down to the 25th through the 27th verses:

"When Jesus saw that a crowd was running to the scene, he rebuked the evil spirit. 'You deaf and mute spirit,' he said, 'I command you, come out of him and never enter him again.'

"The evil spirit shrieked, convulsed him violently and came out. The boy looked so much like a corpse that many said, 'He's dead.' But Jesus took him by the hand and lifted him to his feet, and he stood up."

Now you can imagine how the nine Apostles felt. They were ashamed and embarrassed. They hadn't been able to do a thing for this poor little boy. They'd tried to cast the demon out of him, but it had, in essence, just laughed at them. "Sorry, folks...you can try all you want, but I'm staying right here."

But when Jesus came around, the demon was immediately subject to his authority, and the boy was instantaneously healed.

And so the Apostles wanted to know what they had been doing wrong. Why had the demon refused to obey them?

Jesus responded that this type of demon could only be

driven out through prayer and fasting.

What Jesus was saying is that there are times when you really have to prepare yourself to go into battle. Now I believe that as a Christian you should be prepared to do spiritual battle every day of your life. You should be spending much time in prayer, in reading your Bible, in meditating on God's Word, in fellowshipping with other Christians. You should be doing all of the things that will help to keep you strong spiritually.

But at the same time, there are going to be certain situations that may require extra effort on your part. For example, you may need to pray *and* fast to prepare for a particular conflict or situation.

How will you know when special preparation is required? God will tell you. If you are listening to Him, if you are in tune with the Holy Spirit, you will know what God is saying to you, and you will be ready for anything that comes along. That is why it is so important to spend as much time in prayer as you possibly can. And I don't mean just talking to God. I mean listening to Him, and finding out what it is that He wants to say to you.

As you read through the Gospels, you will find that Jesus prayed a great deal. Many times, he went up onto a mountain, or got away into some other isolated place where He could be alone with His heavenly Father, and prayed all night. You can know for a fact that Jesus wasn't talking all night long. He was listening, too. And sometimes, I'm sure, He was just sitting there, enjoying His Father's presence, and just communing as friend with friend.

Have you ever been in an uncomfortable silence? Perhaps you're with someone you really don't know all that well, and you don't know what to talk to them about — so there's kind of an awkward silence, and you're fumbling around in your mind trying to think of something interesting to say. That's really a difficult situation, isn't it?

On the other hand, there is the kind of deep silence that develops between friends. You can be with someone you truly love, and there's not a word passing between you, but that's okay, because there is a kind of unspoken communication. You can just be together, and be silent together and love one another. Well, that's the sort of relationship we all need to develop with our Heavenly Father. We need to learn to enjoy just sitting with Him, resting with Him, and being ministered to by the joy and peace of His Holy presence. If you don't know what it's like to just be with God that way, then I really feel sorry for you, because being in His presence in that way is one of the greatest experiences imaginable. It is a source of strength, wisdom, peace and joy. It is a means of preparation for the battles that Christians have to face in this world.

Christ spent countless hours with His Father to help prepare Him for all of the battles He faced, right on up to and including His death at the hands of Roman soldiers.

You simply cannot go into war against the forces of hell without being properly prepared.

During the course of my ministry I have come face to face with all sorts of demonic presences and all sorts of manifestations. I have had people foam at the mouth, seen them fall down and slither across the floor, and I've had them growl. I've had them fall to the floor as if they were dead. I've even had people start barking like they were dogs.

But I've never been stopped in my tracks. I've never recoiled in surprise or shock, because I have always been ready and willing to be used of God in any way.

Sometimes, when a demon is being cast out of a person, it's so strong that you can see a knot coming up through the body. I've actually been able to feel the demonic presence moving through the person's body as I prayed for him.

I have also seen instances where the person being set free was left so weak from the experience that he or she had to go to bed for awhile. That's because there was a great battle taking place within that person's body, and a major force being wrenched out of him.

One time, and only one time, a man I was praying for was actually slightly injured by the force of the demon leaving him, and he began to bleed around his mouth.

Why am I telling you all of this? To help you prepare for battle. This is a war we must win, and in order to win it, we have to be prepared for everything the enemy throws at us. That is why it is so important to take a look at how our Lord dealt with demons.

And another important area for study is coming up next. We're going to discuss how the early church reacted against Lucifer's power.

Strong's Concordance #3198

5

THE GATES OF HELL SHALL NOT PREVAIL

Jesus Christ said that the gates of hell would not be able to prevail against His church.

Some people misunderstand that. They turn it around and look at it as if Jesus were saying that the gates of the church would be able to prevail against the forces of hell. In other words, they have a kind of fortress mentality, where the church is standing strong and secure despite an all-out assault against it by the armies of Lucifer.

But that's not the picture Christ was giving us. It's the other way around. It's the church going on the offensive against the forces of evil. When I think about this, I see in my mind a bunch of people with a battering ram, actually crashing down the city gates of hell, and releasing those who are held prisoner there.

This is so important that I can't over-stress it. We are to be the ones who are on the offensive. We are to be the ones who put demons to flight, and not the other way around.

That's the way it was in the church of the first century, and that's the way it ought to be today!

When you read through the Book of Acts, you'll find out that the early church was still doing battle with demon power, even after the Resurrection and Ascension of our Lord — and even after the Holy Spirit was given on the Day of Pentecost. This is important, because there are those Christians who believe that all demons were utterly destroyed by Christ's Resurrection. No...they weren't destroyed. They were defeated, yes, but they were not destroyed. There is a difference. They *will* be destroyed, but that will be when Christ returns to set up His kingdom here on earth. Other Christians believe that when the Holy Spirit came in His fullness, on Pentecost, demonic power was swept away from this planet — but that, too, is an erroneous belief.

I've actually had people tell me that there couldn't possibly have been a manifestation of demons following Christ's atoning work on the cross. But anybody who says anything like that obviously hasn't read carefully through the Book of Acts. Nor has he looked around him to see what's going on in the world today.

But my point is that if the first century church had to deal with demons — and it did — then we can expect that we will have to deal with demons today — and we will.

For example, in the eighth chapter of Acts, verse seven, we find that Philip was preaching the Word of God in Samaria, and that unclean spirits, crying with a loud voice, came out of many of those who were possessed.

I have been asked why demons sometimes cry out as they're being forced to leave the human body they've inhabited. It's because they're afraid of the authority being used against them. They don't want to go. And they know the destruction that awaits them.

Now let's go over to the thirteenth chapter of Acts and read about what happened to Barnabas and Paul when they went to the island of Paphos.

"There they met a Jewish sorcerer and false prophet named Bar-Jesus who was an attendant of the proconsul, Sergius Paulus. The proconsul an intelligent man, sent for Barnabas and Saul because he wanted to hear the word of God. But Elymas, the sorcerer (for that is what his name means) opposed

them and tried to turn the proconsul from the faith. Then Saul, who was also called Paul, filled with the Holy Spirit, looked straight at Elymas and said, 'You are a child of the devil and an enemy of everything that is right! Will you never stop perverting the right ways of the Lord? Now the hand of the Lord is against you. You are going to be blind, and for a time you will be unable to see the light of the sun.'

Acts 13:6-11, NIV

And it happened just like Paul said it would. Immediately, Elymas was unable to see. He had to find somebody to lead him around by the hand.

Now there are a couple of things I want you to see about this particular occurrence. First of all, as a sorcerer, Elymas was undoubtedly in league with all sorts of hellish influences, and well acquainted with demons, so what we have here is an encounter with evil spirits, even though the Scriptures don't say specifically that this is what was going on.

The second thing I want you to see is that the Bible says that Paul looked "straight at Elymas." The King James Version says that he "set his eyes on him." I think that was a divine activity, that in that moment, Paul looked at that man with the eyes of discernment and saw all the evil and deceit and mischief that was in him.

The third thing I want us to see is that Paul was full of the Holy Spirit. He was not acting in His own power, but in the power and might of God.

We need the same things. We need to pray that God will give us the gift of discernment, and we need to be full of the Holy Spirit. We must be yielded to God, and we must have the power and anointing that comes from being baptized by His Holy Spirit.

Are you full of the Holy Spirit? If you aren't, you need to

be. You need to surrender to Him, to ask Him to fill you, empower you and give you all of the gifts He has for you.

DO PEOPLE REALLY WANT TO BE FREE?

Now this encounter between Paul and Elymas raises one important question. Undoubtedly, this sorcerer had a demon or demons within him. So why didn't Paul cast them out? Why did he blast the man himself instead of dealing with the demons that were involved?

I'll tell you why. Because this man was totally open to the demons in his life. He wanted them to be there. He even used them to earn his livelihood as a sorcerer.

And you know, there are people just like that in the world today. They don't *want* to be set free.

What I'm saying, again, is that some people have flat-out sold out to the devil. They haven't been "invaded" by demons. They've taken them in willingly and they don't want to get rid of them. There can be no deliverance for those who do not want in the least to be delivered...and that's what was going on here on the island of Paphos.

Another example of people who were in cahoots with demons is found in the 16th chapter of Acts. In this instance, a young girl who was possessed by "a spirit of divination" began following Paul and Silas around, crying out, "These men are the servants of the Most High God, who proclaim to us the way of salvation." Once again, the demon recognized the authority of the Gospel. It knew who Paul and Silas were and openly admitted it.

Now what this girl was saying wasn't a bad advertisement...but it began to get to Paul because she just wouldn't shut up about it. Everywhere he went, she was right behind him, shouting these things. And instead of attracting people to hear what he had to say, it began to have the opposite effect. Besides that, Paul could feel in his spirit that there was something wrong here. What the girl was saying was right, but it just didn't feel right inside. There was something evil about it even though the words were true. So finally, Paul had just had enough, and he commanded the evil spirit to come out of her. Which it did, of course.

Well, what happened next? Was everybody happy that this poor girl, who had been in bondage for so long, had been set free?

Not at all! In fact, just the opposite was true.

First of all, the girl was a slave, and her owners had made quite a bit of money off of her — getting her to tell fortunes for people and so on. Well, they realized right away that they had lost their meal ticket, and they weren't at all happy about it. In fact, they got the whole town riled up against Paul and Silas, so much so that the local magistrates sentenced them to be beaten with rods. And then, after they had been severely beaten, they were thrown into prison, and the jailer was commanded to keep them locked up securely.

Isn't that crazy? Wouldn't you think that the townspeople would look at this girl, and see that she was smiling and happy, and free from demonic possession, and beg Paul and Silas to pray for them? Wouldn't you think they'd say, "We see what you've done for this poor girl — now won't you please do the same thing for us?"

But a mob mentality took over. People were frightened by what had happened. And they didn't like outsiders coming in and "messing up" the status quo...and the result was trouble for Paul and Silas.

Don't ever think the world will be on your side if you are doing battle against the forces of hell. Many times the world will fight you just as hard as the demons do.

But even here, God was able to use the situation for good. I'm not going to spend time talking about it here, but if you'll go on and read the rest of that chapter, you'll see that God used the incident to bring about the salvation of the jailer and his entire household.

Moving on to the nineteenth chapter, we find a rather humorous story about some people who were going around trying to cast out evil spirits in the name of Jesus, but who didn't really know Jesus at all. These fellows had apparently seen Paul casting out demons in the name of Jesus, and decided that they'd do the same thing.

They came to a man who was possessed with a particularly violent spirit, and commanded that the spirit come out of him, "In the name of Jesus, whom Paul preaches."

Well, they were attempting to use the name of the Lord like it was some sort of lucky charm, and it isn't. They might as well have been saying "hocus pocus" instead of "in the name of Jesus." Yes, yes, yes, there is power and might in the very name of Jesus. But it is not to be trifled with. It is not a toy. It is not a magic charm.

And so the Bible says that the man with the demon replied, *"Jesus I know, and Paul I know, but who are you?"* (Acts 19:15) Then he jumped on them, tearing at their clothes and beating them so severely that the Bible says, "they ran out of the house naked and bleeding."

It's quite a scene isn't it? It's a funny picture to think of those men, running down the road as fast as they could, and thinking, "We sure won't try that again!"

CAST DOWN BY REPUTATION

I've talked before about Lester Sumrall. He is someone I particularly admire because he is not afraid of the truth. He tells it the way it is no matter what anyone else thinks. And, he has seen hundreds of people set free from enslavement by demons.

I have heard him talk about the time when he was driving a demon out of a man, and the demon spoke to him and said, "I know who you are. We've heard of you."

Have the demons heard of you? If you are living for God you can bet they've heard of you, because you are a threat to them. If you are aware of their existence, and if you are willing to take them on with the power and might of Jesus they've heard of you because they are afraid of you! Wouldn't it be a great thing to hear from the mouth of a demon, "I know who you are. You're the one who beats us everywhere we go. You're the one who has destroyed so many of us!"

That's the way it *can* and *should* be for you.

But you have to know where your authority lies. You can't take it lightly. It isn't a game to go up against the worst that hell has to offer. And when I consider that, I'd have to say that the men who were beaten up by this demon-possessed man were actually lucky to escape with their lives. They were embarrassed and bruised, yes. But at least they were still living and breathing!

Now before we conclude this look at the early church's battles against the forces of evil, I want to look at two more verses of scripture. The first is from the sixth chapter of Ephesians (NKJ), verses 10-12. There we read, from the hand of the Apostle Paul:

> *"Finally, my brethren, be strong in the Lord and in the power of His might.*
>
> *"Put on the whole armor of God, that you may be able to stand against the wiles of the devil.*
>
> *"For we do not wrestle against flesh and blood, but against principalities, against powers, against the rulers of the darkness of this age, against spiritual hosts of wickedness in the heavenly places."*

Notice that Paul doesn't say, "be weak and confused, and have small faith." Of course not! He is calling us to a position of authority, and active opposition to the schemes of the evil ones.

WHAT ARE WE UP AGAINST?

I'd like you to re-read that verse again, and notice all the times the word "against" is used. What are we going up "against?"

First of all, Paul makes clear that we are not fighting against flesh and blood. There is more than human strength here. This is a supernatural battle. What we *are* wrestling against, first of all, is "principalities."

That means that we are going up against the rulers of evil — against princes who have been set up to reign over territories and regions and, as we've discussed previously, over cities. We are not to stand aside and let these wicked beings take over our communities. We are to stand up and do battle against them!

Number two, we are against "powers." There are evil powers at loose in this world, and we are, once again, called to "stand" against them.

Thirdly, we are against *"the rulers of the darkness of this age."* We are against the darkness and for the light. Jesus calls us to be the "light of the world." We want to walk in the light and we want to bring others into the light. Sometimes you might start to talk to a person, to perhaps share with them about Christ, and you can sense that there's something wrong. That person is ensnared by darkness and needs to be brought into the light.

Finally, we also wrestle "against spiritual hosts of wickedness in the heavenly places."

Remember what we talked about before, that there are different types of "heavens." In this instance, Paul is referring to the "heaven" where spirits dwell. The Living Bible says that we are wrestling *"against huge numbers of wicked spirits in the spirit world."*

And that's the truth. There are vast numbers of demons in this universe, but remember what I've told you. If you have the power of God within you, all of the forces of hell are no match for you. You could be out in the middle of the sea in a little bitty rowboat, and be surrounded by all of Lucifer's battleships. He could have every one of his huge guns on you. He could be sending his bombers and his fighter planes over your head. They could be bombing you and strafing you with machine gun fire, and doing everything in the world to destroy you. But as long as you have the Holy Spirit with you in that little boat, Lucifer's forces won't even be able to mess up your hair!

Praise God for His power and might, and for letting that power and might flow through His children.

The second of the two verses I want us to see is James 4:7: *"Therefore, submit to God. Resist the devil and he will flee from you,"* (New King James)

These are two important ways every believer can obtain power over the devil and his armies. First, be submitted to God. If you are yielded to Him you will be under His protecting arm, and the devil will have a dickens of a time trying to get through to you!

Active, strong resistance is the second way to defeat old Lucifer. When he comes at you and tries to get you to do something you know you shouldn't do, simply say, "No!" Tell him, "I refuse to listen to you, and I won't do what you want me to do. In Jesus name, I break your power."

How much better off this world would be, the church would be, if people would simply learn to resist the devil.

Unfortunately, some people sit around and think about temptation. They ponder and think about what might happen if they just did this one little thing here. And before they know what hit them, they're involved in some full-blown sin, and they're wide open for an army of demons to take up residence in them.

The simplest way to defeat the devil is just to say no to him in the name of Jesus. If you do that on a consistent basis, you will begin to build up resistance and you will find it easier and easier to overcome his temptations.

And, what's more, his temptations will come less and less frequently!

Unfortunately, some people have never resisted a temptation in their life! In the next chapter, I'm going to be talking to some of those people, as we discuss, "Seven Steps to Demon Possession."

6

SEVEN STEPS TO DEMON POSSESSION

Some people invite demons into their lives. They get involved in witchcraft or magic, or whatever you want to call it, and they willingly yield themselves to Lucifer and his demons. They draw chalk outlines on the floor, and say strange incantations, and flat-out give themselves over to demon control.

Other people invite demons into their lives in a less blatant way. They get involved in sins — drinking, taking drugs, promiscuous sexual activity, and so on — and because of the lifestyle they've chosen, they wind up with a host of demons taking up residence in their bodies.

And then there are other people who, though they may be well-meaning, become entrapped by demons through the seven steps I want to talk about in this chapter.

We're going to spend some time looking at each of these seven steps, but before we do that, I just want to tell you what the seven steps are:

1) Regression.

2) Repression.

3) Suppression.

4) Depression.

5) Oppression.

6) Obsession.

7) Possession.

Now let's take a closer look at each of these seven steps.

REGRESSION

To regress means to withdraw, to decrease or backslide. It also means to revert to a former level, to reverse a trend or to shift to a lower state.

If you are regressing, you are moving backwards. A person who is regressing is likely to be a luke-warm Christian. He is one of those whom Jesus said He will "spew" out of his mouth.

This person might follow a path something like this:

He was making spiritual progress...reading his Bible and praying, and spending time with the Lord. But then he was too tired to study the Bible one day, didn't bother to pray the next day, and before he realized it, he wasn't spending any time at all with God. And so he began to lose what progress he had made. His spiritual muscles began to atrophy and turn to flab, and he became easy pickings for demonic power.

To understand regression, we need to take a look at the opposite word, which is *progression*. If you are not moving forward, you are probably moving backward. In other words, if you're not *progressing*, you are probably *regressing*.

Look around at some of the so-called "mainline" Christian churches. Those churches were formed in the fires of revival. Some of them were a reaction to the corruption of the church. Sound doctrine had been perverted, the Gospel was not being preached, and so brave men put their lives on the line in order to change things. There was a time when the Spirit of God burned brightly in those churches.

But look at them today and some of them are spiritually dead. They're social clubs where most of the people don't even remember why it is they're getting together on Sunday morning. What happened? Somewhere along the line they quite progressing and began regressing, and now they find themselves in a sad, sad condition.

You know, when the communists took over Russia, they closed down some of the churches there and turned them into museums. And that was a terrible thing. But when I look around me, I can see some churches right here in America that are, in reality, nothing more than museums. They're not useful for anything except perhaps for the beauty of their stained-glass windows or their ornate furniture.

Regression is the first avenue by which Satan takes over any human soul, church, ministry, or what-have-you.

Already I've mentioned Lester Sumrall several times in this book. That's because he has so much wisdom to share, and because he is such a wonderful example of godly living.

One time when I was having lunch with him, he said, "I live a progressive life."

I said, "Yes, sir," which is pretty much all you ever say when Brother Sumrall is talking to you.

"You know," he went on, "a lot of my friends are old and in their rocking chairs. We started out in ministry about the same time. But I'm still going strong and they're totally in a regressive state of living."

Again, "Yes, sir." It was the truth.

And then he said, "And I want that in you."

"Great!" I said. "Give it to me!"

He laughed and said, "Well, it doesn't quite come like that. It comes by decisions that you make. And it comes because of how you deal with the challenges of life, and the demonic attacks on you."

He went on to explain the difference between regression and progression this way: "To regress in the human personality is to go backward in spiritual force and power. The human person is built for progressive life, an advancing life, and an understanding life."

He told me that he kept on the move because he wanted to be progressive. He had made the decision as to how he was going to live.

"I'm not going to retire. I'm going to leave when it's time."

A regressive person may start to retire years before it's actually time for him to retire. He gives up his goals and gets relaxed, and just sort of "fades away." Remember what General Douglas MacArthur said? "Old soldiers never die. They just fade away." Well, there is no "fading away" in the kingdom of God.

When the righteous grow old, their day gets brighter and brighter, and not dimmer and dimmer.

This is important, once again, because it is the very first way Satan is able to make inroads into the human soul.

Second Corinthians 3:17-18 has some things to say about the person who is *progressing* as he should:

"Now the Lord is the Spirit; and where the Spirit of the Lord is, there is liberty.

"But we all, with unveiled face, beholding as in a mirror the glory of the Lord, are being transformed into the same image from glory to glory, just as by the Spirit of the Lord." (NKJ)

First of all, in order to make progress, there has to be liberty. Where there is a spirit of liberty, you can feel free to release yourself to the presence of God, and to let His Spirit minister to you.

Some churches are so fossilized that every Sunday service is the same. There is no liberty, and the Spirit has been quenched. I think it's important to do things decently and in order, to have a plan that you're going to follow. But sometimes, the Spirit wants you to discard your plan. He has something else in mind. It's important to have the freedom to follow wherever it is the Lord wants to lead you. Such liberty brings progression. A lack of liberty brings regression.

Now I love this part about being transformed from "glory to glory." In other words, it may be glorious right now, but just you wait, because it's going to be even more glorious later on. Don't ever think that you've reached the summit. If you get to the point where you think you've got it made, or that God has given you everything He has to give you, that's the day you stop striving to move forward, and the day you start sliding back down the hill. Don't ever stop "hungering and thirsting" after righteousness. Don't ever stop wanting more of God or of His Holy Spirit.

He has so much to show us and teach us, and it is totally ridiculous for any of us to think that we've gotten to the point that we don't need anything else from Him.

Another thing about a progressive person is that he is interested in others. He is outgoing in the sense that he is willing to give of himself, and that he wants to get to know people. The regressive person is likely to retreat into his own little corner of the world. He's so much "into" himself, that he *can't* show interest in anybody else. Now which one of these people, do you suppose, will be a greater influence for the kingdom of God? Which one will attract people to himself, so that he, in turn, can show them the way to Jesus. It is the man who is progressive, of course.

If you want to be a blessing to people and lead them to Jesus, you have to have an adventurous, progressive attitude.

How can you know if you are falling into a pattern of regression? There are four ways:

1) You will notice that the things that used to bring you excitement and joy no longer do so.

You used to be excited when new people came into your church, but now it doesn't make you feel that way. You used to find an excitement in reading the scriptures — as if

God were speaking directly to you, but now you have to struggle to keep your mind on what you're reading. You used to love to go to church, you couldn't wait for the Sunday morning service, but now it's a chore to drag yourself out of bed. When you sense that all of these things are happening in your life, it's time for you to turn your heart toward God. Ask him to restore to you your first love. Tell him you're sorry for your coldness, and ask Him to give you back your passion.

You have become careless about your commitment to Christ and your goals to help build God's kingdom.

I have had the experience of meeting excited young ministers, who are just bubbling with excitement over all the things they want to do for God and the furthering of His kingdom. Then, I meet the same people a year later, and they've totally forgotten all of those goals. What happened? They got so "busy" with the smaller matters that they forgot all about the larger matters. They got careless. They got the attitude that, "If I don't do it, somebody else will." And that's a regressive attitude. It's the beginning of a long slide downhill.

3) The third way a person can begin to tell that he's regressing is that he begins to see his own excuses as more powerful than his faith.

If you have faith in God, you can come through any challenge that's set before you. Something may look impossible, but you know that all things are possible with God, and so you just keep moving, right through that stone mountain if you have to.

But when you begin to regress, you think, "I'll never be able to do that! Who do I think I am to be able to get that done?" And then you start to make excuses.

"I'm too old," or "I'm too poor," or "I'm too young in the faith." When you realize that your excuses have become the size of giants, and you need a microscope to examine your faith — then you have really fallen into a regressive state of mind.

4) Finally, the fourth way you can tell that you are becoming regressive is that you are ruled more by your feelings than by making decisions and sticking with them. If you don't feel like doing something so you don't do it, you are regressing. If you don't feel like doing something, but you keep pushing forward because you've made a decision to do it, then you are progressing.

Now that we've discussed some of the characteristics of the regressive lifestyle, I want to turn things around and very briefly give you the three characteristics of a progressive person:

1) A progressive person has a willingness to change. He's not tied to old ways of doing things. He is free to follow the Spirit of God wherever He may lead. That willingness to change may include the way that person looks at the Word of God. He may find, as he continues to study the Word, that He needs to change his thinking on a few points. Now some people won't do that. You can sit there, and show them, in black and white, that they have erroneous thinking about something — they can read it for themselves, but they'll tell you, "I see what it says there, but I don't really care, because that's not what I believe." We *all* have to be willing to grow and learn, to accept new understandings that the Lord may give to us.

2) A progressive person has a love for truth and a teachable spirit. This person wants to know the truth, and won't settle for anything less than the truth. He doesn't become defensive if an older, wiser brother or sister tries to instruct him in some way. A regressive person, on the other hand, is likely to become defensive. He says, "Who are you to try to teach me? I know what I'm doing, so just leave me alone!"

3) A progressive person is a strong person in several

ways. He has a strong vision, a strong commitment, has a strong spirit and strong relationships with his brothers and sisters in Christ.

REPRESSION

Let's move on now to the second of the seven steps toward demonic possession, which is Repression.

Lester Sumrall says, "It is most interesting to me that God makes every human being full of expression. The moment a baby is born, the doctor spanks the baby. He's looking for expression. If he doesn't get the expression from the child, he pronounces the baby dead. God desires exuberant expression from all of us."

Sometimes when I'm preaching I might get kind of loud, and even shout a little bit. That's because I'm giving expression to the way I feel, and to the things I want to say.

I may even dance or jump a little. Hallelujah! That's expression!

If I wanted to shout, but whispered instead, that would be repression. If I wanted to jump and dance a little bit because the presence of God had made me excited, but instead I stood there like I was a cigar-store Indian, that would be repression. And as I repressed my feelings, my joy and excitement, that joy and excitement would begin to fade away.

Clarence Darrow was a brilliant lawyer who also happened to be an outspoken atheist. You may remember that he opposed William Jennings Bryan in the Scopes Monkey Trial.

Well, Darrow was a great one for giving advice, and one of the bits of advice he gave went something like this:

If you're going on a trip by train and you find out that you can sit either by a cold-blooded killer or a fundamentalist Christian, be sure to choose the cold-blooded killer for the warmth.

We Christians read that and tend to grimace, or to think about what a blasphemous man Clarence Darrow must have been. But you know what? There was some painful truth in that statement.

Throughout history, too many God-fearing people thought it was wrong to give expression to the joy and happiness God had given them. They went around with long faces, frowning all the time and looking like they'd been sucking on lemons.

What happened was that they began to quench God's Holy Spirit. They became joyless, lifeless and pathetic.

And that's the sort of thing repression does to people.

In one sense, repression may be the outward sign that regression is taking place on the inside.

If you don't laugh anymore, it may be because you've lost your joy. If you don't dance or shout anymore when God's presence floods into the room, it's probably because you don't get excited like you used to.

It really can go both ways. Repression can cause regression to begin to take place. But on the other hand, regression can be what causes repression. You may have to stop and think about all of that for a few moments — but it's important to understand these things.

Some people have a problem with repression because they were raised in a house where they were never allowed to show their feelings. They might even be the type of people who wait to see what everyone else thinks before they let you know what they think about something. If that's how it is with you, then you need to ask God to give you freedom of expression.

Maybe you've been hurt. Maybe you've lost a job, or an important friend, or even a spouse. When something like that happens to you, it's okay to mourn. In fact, you wouldn't be human if you *didn't* mourn. But there is a time for mourning, and then there is a time for getting your life back on track and moving on into the future. Some people allow themselves to get so down, and so defeated and so sad, that they are easy prey for demonic influences. A person who is always feeling sad and defeated is a person who is weak and easily overcome, and that's just what demons are looking for.

It's important for us not only to understand repression when we see it in ourselves, but when we see it in others as well. Sometimes all it takes to change things is to go up to that sad person, and give him a hug and tell him that you appreciate him or love him. Maybe all he needs is someone to talk to. Just having a friend can make such a difference in someone's life, and it can stop them from falling into demonic oppression and possession.

It's funny how people react to things. At Christmas time, for example, some people are excited and full of joy and happiness. They absolutely *love* the Christmas season and everything associated with it. And then there are others who are *so* sad, and so downhearted at Christmas. They walk around with lumps in their throats and tears in their eyes.

We need to strive to be people who find joy in everything God has done for us. But we also need to strive to be people who bring God's comfort and joy to those who are struggling, for whatever reason, with unhappiness. Let's do everything within our power to help lift them out of that state.

God wants exuberant expression from us. He wants us to be able to shout for joy, and to tell him in word and deed that we love Him.

If you try to shout "Hallelujah" or give a hearty "Amen" in some churches they'll tell you to shut up. They don't want you to be free to express yourselves. But that stifling spirit is wrong, and harmful and must be avoided!

When I think of expressiveness I think of heaven.

Imagine what that's going to be like, with all of the angels and all of the saved from every nation gathered around the throne and singing and praising God with all of our hearts! It's really going to be something, isn't it?! But, really, we ought to be working toward the establishment of a little bit of heaven on earth. We ought to worship God here in just the same way we're going to worship him there, and that means giving expression to our most joyful and grateful emotions!

I watch some people coming into the worship service on Sunday morning, and it's amazing how they'll change once the service starts. They're smiling and laughing and visiting with their friends, and their kids are happy...but then the worship starts and they get the longest, weariest expressions! And they're forcing their children to be stiff and straight! That's not the way it ought to be.

It's the devil who wants us to be cold and stiff and emotionless, *not* God!

I was in a church once and they had this big sign up in front that quoted from Scripture, "The Lord is in His holy temple; let all the earth keep silence before him." The idea was that people were supposed to come into the building and sit down and be as quiet as church mice. But, you know, as well-intentioned as the people may have been who put that sign up, I think they were dead wrong. One of the things I like to hear in a congregation prior to the start of the worship service, is a loud buzz of happy conversation.

I like it because it's a sign that the people really love each other. They're happy to see each other, they're sharing the latest news with one another, they're talking about all the good things the Lord has done in their lives since they've last seen each other. And that's great! It's an indication that people are excited about what God has been doing in their lives!

Certainly, once the worship service starts, I don't want

that buzz of conversation to continue. I want the people to give their full attention to the service, but I want them to do it with the same sort of enthusiasm they had when they were greeting each other earlier.

When we express our excitement and joy regarding what God has done in our lives, Lucifer and his demons simply cannot stand to be around us. They don't want to hear it. But when we repress those feelings, the demon forces think, "Ah, that's better. I can live with this." And, unfortunately, that's oftentimes what they do.

Not too long ago, I had the chance to visit Israel. And when you go to Israel and see some of the holy sites there, it's really silly to tiptoe around and whisper in hushed tones. Instead, those are the very places where you need to lift your voices and your hearts in praise to God for what he has done for you! Some people won't like it? That's okay. God likes it, and He's really the only one who matters!

Too many of today's churches are not giving joyful expression to what God is doing. They are not concentrating on the positive, but instead, they are focusing most of their attention on the negatives. They are criticizing some preacher or evangelist because they don't like the way he says things — never mind the fact that he's bringing healing and deliverance to hundreds or thousands of people.

Someone says, "Did you see that crippled man get up out of his wheelchair at last night's service?"

"Oh, well, sure I did. But I didn't think the sermon was all that great."

Some people worry about the way the evangelist combs his hair, or the way he pronounces certain words. They think he's too dramatic or too flamboyant or too slick or too whatever else you can think of. But none of those things matter. The important thing to think about is, "Are people being ministered to? Are they being saved? Are they being healed and set free from demonic oppression and possession?" If they are, then our response should be to praise God joyfully and perhaps even noisily for what he is doing in our midst. God wants us to *express*, not *repress* our feelings.

I believe that if there's anything a demon likes better than a blatant sinner, it's a Christian with a negative, critical attitude. He can do more harm with that kind of Christian, you see, because he can sow dissension within the church of God. I've seen him use people like that to actually split churches apart. Some people got so disgusted they just walked away and said, "If that's what Christianity is all about, then I don't want anything to do with it." Churches have withered on the vine because of such negativism. They've been completely drained of their evangelistic zeal. They've forgotten and forsaken the calling that was on them, and they might as well nail their doors shut.

Let me give one more example of the way repression can work to damage the human spirit — an example I think we can all understand.

What happens when a young man and woman fall in love and get married? One of the things that happens is that they are constantly telling each other how much they love and care for each other. They do it because they're so much in love they really can't help themselves. "I love you," is said often, and with great passion.

The young man may even tell his bride, "I'll never let a day go by without telling you how much I love you."

And he means it when he says it.

But as the years go by, and things begin to get in the way, that couple's expression of love for each other comes less and less frequently. They don't say, "I love you" very much, and because they don't, the feelings that they once had begin to cool off. The wife says to her husband, "You never tell me you love me anymore!" And because she says it in an accusing way, her husband snaps back with an "I love you," that really sounds like, "Give me a break! I'm tired today."

What has happened, you see, is that they have allowed their feelings for one another to fade away. If they had actually done what they promised they would do — if the man never would have let a day go by without telling his wife how much he loved her, and if the wife had done the same, they most likely would have been able to keep their love alive. Because they didn't express their feelings, the feelings eventually began to go away.

That happens again and again in our society. No wonder the divorce rate is so high!

Do you love God? Then tell Him. Are you grateful for what He's done in your life? Let Him know. If you repress your feelings, you are bound to grow cold, indifferent, and you will attract unwanted demonic influences.

So don't let anything hold you back from expressing your love for God and your joy over what he has done for you.

SUPPRESSION

The third of the seven steps along the road to demon possession is Suppression.

The dictionary defines suppression as "to squeeze down abnormally." Suppression also means to conceal, as to suppress information, feelings and desires.

You can see that suppression is closely related to repression, but there is a difference. That is that repression is primarily something we do to ourselves, for various reasons. Suppression, on the other hand, is something that comes from outside. It is the beginning of demonic inroads being made into a person's life, and it needs to be broken by the power of God.

Here's an example of suppression:

Suppose you're in a worship service, and you clearly sense that God is talking to you. He has something He wants you to share with the other people who are there. But you just sit there, with your mouth shut. You feel like your insides are going to explode because you want so badly to open your mouth and give this Word that God is speaking to you — but you just can't do it!

You might even try to do it, but you can't get your mouth to open. It's like one of those dreams you used to have when you were a kid, when a bad guy is coming after you, and you try to run, but your legs just won't work. Part of the reason you can't do what you want to do is that the devil is whispering to you, telling you that you're not *really* hearing from God, or that the other people are going to reject what you have to say.

That's one form of suppression.

It may come in many other ways. Perhaps you have a strong desire to do this thing or that thing for God, but something is always holding you back. You have a tremendous desire to be used in some type of service for God's kingdom, but when it gets right down to it, it just doesn't happen.

I know a man who has always wanted to be a missionary to Latin America. When he was in college, he learned how to speak Spanish fluently so that he could be more effective as a missionary. He learned everything there is to know about Latin American culture. He went to seminary so he could get a thorough grounding in God's Word.

But that was nearly 40 years ago. And you know what? He's never made it to the mission field, and by this time in his life, I think it's pretty safe to say that he never will. He's done all right in life, really, but he's lived in constant disappointment because he has not done the one thing he was certain he was supposed to do, the one thing he really wanted to do.

Why didn't he ever make it to South America? Because of suppression. Something was always squeezing his desires and stopping him before he could follow through. That's what Satan can do to you if you give in to suppression.

Suppression cannot be defeated through will power, or by trying harder. But it can be defeated and broken by direct action, by taking authority over it in the name of Jesus.

DEPRESSION

Depression is a broken spirit. A person who is depressed is a person who has been pressed down to the point where his spirit was crushed.

We all become depressed from time to time. Life in this world can sometimes get us down for a variety of reasons. Just taking a look at the evening news or reading the morning newspaper is enough to give you a mild dose of depression. But that ought to fade away when we remember that no matter what happens in the world, and no matter what happens in our individual lives, God is still on the throne. He is still in charge, and He is working everything out for the good of those who love Him, as it says in Romans 8:28.

For some people, that realization doesn't help. Depression grabs hold of them and will not let them go. One chronically depressed person told me that he had reached the point where there was no joy in anything he did. All of the things that had once given him pleasure were just dead to him. He was going through the motions and that was all. He felt that there was nothing worthwhile in his life, not even his family.

You can see why a person like that would be an easy mark for demonic forces — who are always on the prowl, looking for someone they can sink their teeth, or fangs, into.

King David was someone who knew about depression.

Look at Psalm 42:5:

"Why are you downcast, O my soul?

"Why so disturbed within me?

"Put your hope in God

"For I will yet praise Him,

"My Savior and my God."

David became depressed, but when he did, he chased it away by concentrating on the greatness and goodness of God. He praised God even when he may not have felt much like it, and his "downcast" soul was lifted up when he did.

Let's take a look now at some of the causes of depression.

LEGALISTIC RELIGION CAN CAUSE DEPRESSION BY BRINGING PEOPLE UNDER CONDEMNATION

There is a form of religion that seeks to control people and, in doing so, takes away their freedom. Legalistic religion says, "You have to do exactly what we tell you to do." In essence, that's saying, "We want you to look to us for guidance in religious matters, and *not* to God." No wonder people become depressed when they are living in that kind of bondage.

TRADITIONS CAN CAUSE DEPRESSION

For example, it is natural to grieve over the death of a loved one, even if you know that loved one has gone on to be with God. Separation is very difficult, even when you're certain there's going to be a reunion someday — but it's possible to take it much too far. For example, some people have a tradition that they must wear black for a year, and that they're being "unfaithful" to the deceased if they so much as crack a smile, and so on. Traditions like that aren't good for anyone. They unnaturally prolong the grieving process and they can lead you down into the valley of depression. If you don't allow yourself to grieve, it will come out some other way in your life, so go ahead and grieve, but realize that it is only for a season, and then it's time to put it away and get on with your life. When a person grieves beyond the natural period of time, then the spirit of grief will come in and take control, and the result can be severe, debilitating depression.

DEPRESSION MAY BE TRIGGERED BY OTHER FORMS OF LOSS OR TROUBLE

Getting laid off from your job can bring about depression, of course. Financial trouble can bring about depression — not being able to pay your bills and getting harassing phone calls from people you owe. Having a child rebel against you can bring about depression (as it did with King David). Having a friend turn against you, or the breaking up of a romantic relationship can cause severe depression.

As I said, it's understandable why some of these things should bring on a state of depression, but it's not understandable why anyone would want to give in to it and live like that. And yet, my own experience tells me that that is exactly what happens with some folks. Some people actually enjoy being depressed, and when you sense that that's the case, it's a pretty sure sign of demonic involvement. It's sad to say, but some people seem to be professionally depressed. It's how they get attention. And when that's how they are, there's not much of anything anyone can do to help them.

I have known people that were in constant need of cheering words and prayer, who wanted every bit of attention I could give them...but none of it did a bit of good. They were depressed and that's how they wanted to stay.

Remember that for a person to gain victory over depression he has to *want* to be victorious. We talked in the last chapter about how some people don't want to be delivered from demons because they like having demons in their life. Well, it's the same thing here. Some people can't be helped because they don't want to be helped. But help is always available for those who want it.

If depression seems to be gaining the upper hand over you, there are several things you can do to shake it off.

The first thing you can do is, of course, to pray. Ask God to help you get out from under this thing. And praise Him for His greatness and goodness. Remember that the Bible teaches that God inhabits the praises of His people, and depression cannot exist in the presence of the Living God.

You can also take authority over the spirit of depression, and break its power through the name and authority of Jesus.

And then there are some natural things you can do to break depression's grip. Sometimes you just need a change of scenery.

Get up and leave the room. Go do something different. You may not feel like it, but that doesn't matter. Do it anyway. A depressed person is likely to want to sit in his room and stare at the wall. That's no good, because it allows depression to feed upon itself. So get up, get dressed, go out and do something. It might be that a simple change of your environment or routine is the very thing you need to begin to win the battle.

If you're severely depressed, one thing you cannot afford to do is to cut yourself off from your brothers and sisters in the Lord. I understand that when depression hits, you may want to close yourself off, and that you don't feel like being around people who are happy and full of joy. But that's exactly what you need. God knows that it's important for us to spend as much time as possible with other believers. There is a strength in numbers, and a release that comes from being surrounded by people of faith — people who will pray with you, minister to you, and love you back from depression.

We all need to live up to what the Apostle Paul wrote in the sixth chapter and second verse of Galatians, when he told us that we are to carry each other's burdens. When we really do that, we will always make short work of depression.

The devil would love it if every Christian in the world were depressed. He knows that people who are depressed are not energetic or enthusiastic about anything. They are generally lethargic and apathetic, and easily defeated. A depressed person becomes listless, inactive and disinterested in what goes on around him or her — and that means big trouble in the life of a Christian. If Satan could get enough Christians to give in to depression, he would have free reign on this planet. He wouldn't have anyone to oppose him or to bind him, and he would be running roughshod over *everyone.*

Now if you are really a strong Christian, you can break depression's hold over you all by yourself. But most people need help when it moves in on them. And if you need help, then by all means ask for it. I've known Christians who were too proud to ask for the help they needed, because they didn't want to appear weak. But it is far, far better to admit your weakness than to play games while the life is sapped right out of you.

Besides, we all need help from time to time, and that's precisely why the Lord gave us to each other!

Basically, though, a good response to depression is to just say, "No you don't, in Jesus name," and swat that demon back over the fence like you're hitting a tennis ball. And then, get involved in what's going on in your church. People used to say, "Idle hands are the devil's workshop." In a lot of ways, that's true. Stay busy in the Lord, and depression won't be able to get its talons into you.

Let's move on now to the fifth of the seven steps into demonic control.

THE FIFTH STEP IS OPPRESSION

Oppression is like depression carried to the Nth degree. To oppress someone means to weigh them down with a load they're not capable of carrying.

As a biblical example, consider the children of Israel, who were being oppressed by the Pharaoh. God looked down and had pity on them. He heard their mourning and saw their tears, and He sent Moses and Aaron to deliver them.

In the same way, some people today are being oppressed by demons who condemn them, who load them up with false guilt, and who keep whispering to them, "You're no good! God couldn't possibly love you." Are you weighed down by your past sins and failures? Then you are being oppressed.

I ask, "Don't you realize that Jesus Christ paid the price for your sins? That they've been washed away by His blood?"

"Oh, yes," comes the reply. "I know in my head that that's true, but I have a hard time getting it down into my heart."

Or someone else says, "But you don't know the things I've done. I want to believe I'm forgiven...but I just *can't.*"

Brothers and sisters, if you are struggling with those kinds of feelings, then you are a victim of oppression, and you need to deal with it before it deals with you!

One of the ways Christians can fall into oppression is through sickness.

Take a look at Acts 10:38, and you'll see that during Jesus' earthly ministry, He went about healing those who were oppressed by the devil. We see from this passage that people who are sick can become oppressed by their illness.

For example, think about someone who has just been told by his doctor that he has cancer. Almost immediately, that person will start thinking that he's going to die. Even if it's a minor thing — something that can be easily treated — the very word, "cancer" can nearly destroy a person.

People who have a serious, long-term illness are often extremely oppressed. They're oppressed because they're worried about the future: Will I get well? Will I be able to pay my medical bills? What will happen to my family if I don't get well? Am I going to suffer?

With all of these thoughts running through your mind, of course you're going to be oppressed.

But there is a solution — a solution that is found in Matthew 11:28-30:

> *"Come to Me, all you who labor and are heavy laden, and I will give you rest. Take my yoke upon you and learn from Me, for I am gentle and lowly in heart, and you will find rest for your souls. For My yoke is easy and My burden is light."*

In those words of Jesus, we find the answer for every person who is oppressed by the devil.

Some of us try to carry too much on our own shoulders. We worry, we fret, we run here and there as fast as we can, doing things *for* the Lord. But we don't let Him help us. We don't come to Him with our burdens and our cares and let Him work through us. And so we wind up depressed and oppressed.

In his book, *They Speak With Other Tongues*, John Sherill tells the story of what happened when he was asked to sing in a church choir. Sherill, according to his own estimation, wasn't a great talent as a singer...but the choir needed some bass voices, so there he was. When he expressed his misgivings, one of the "real" singers gave him some advice.

"Just lean into me while we're singing," he said.

That's what Sherill did, and to his surprise, he heard his own voice booming forth in clear, deep, bass tones. It was almost as if Sherill's voice were being amplified and carried by the energy that was coming from the other singer. Now I don't know enough about sound and how it travels to give you the scientific principle behind that experience. I just take the author's word for the fact that it happened. And the application is clear. Lean into the Lord, and you will be surprised at what He is able to do through you. Don't do things *for* the Lord. Let Him work *through* you to accomplish His purposes.

They say that famous evangelist Dwight L. Moody spent at least one hour in prayer every morning. Except, that is, when he knew he was facing an extremely busy day. Then he spent *two* hours in prayer. There was a man who understood the importance of leaning on God.

Show me a man or woman who knows how to lean on the Lord, and I'll show you a man or woman who is *not* oppressed!

The servant of God should not strive. He should not be driven by ambition. His desire should be to obey God in every aspect of life and, otherwise, to rest in God's loving care.

Oppression is a terrible thing. It can be such a heavy weight hanging over people that it even prevents them from believing the Scriptures. For example, I have gone to pray for sick people and quickly discovered that they were under a spirit of oppression that was so heavy they couldn't believe what the Word of God has to say about healing. I'd show them that healing was provided for in the sacrifice of Christ and they'd say, "Well, I can see that it says that. But are you sure that's what it means?"

In a situation like that, the only thing I could do was to take authority over the spirit of oppression.

I'll tell them, "I break this power over you. I command that this oppression be broken in the name of Jesus. Now spirit man, inside of him, stand up! Stand up and realize that Jesus will carry your burdens and heal you of all your diseases."

Once that spirit of oppression has been broken, it's much easier for a person to believe and be healed.

We've seen that sickness can be a cause of oppression. Fear can also bring about a spirit of oppression.

Some people live in fear. They're afraid they'll lose their jobs. They're afraid nobody will like them. They're afraid they'll go broke. They're afraid they'll get sick. They're afraid of the past. They're afraid of the future. I don't care what it is. You name it and somebody is afraid of it.

If you're living in that kind of fear, then you're being oppressed by a devil, and you need to take authority over it!

People who are bound up by fear have made the mistake of listening to Lucifer's lies. "You're going to die tomorrow." "Your job is going to be phased out." "Your wife is going to fall out of love with you." And on and on he goes. He is the father of lies and he never gets tired of telling them.

I had a person come to me for prayer who had lived out in the world for years, actively involved in sexual perversion. He said to me, "I'm saved and spirit-filled now, and my life is together and I'm serving God, but I have a fear that because of the way I lived, AIDS is going to get me."

I said, "Look at me." (I wanted to be sure he was hearing everything I said to him.) Then I told him, "You don't have to worry about AIDS. It's not going to get you."

"Well...how do you know that?"

"Because," I said, "God is in control of your life. He is in control of that situation. If you've come to Jesus and you've given your life to God and you've asked Him to cleanse you, He'll also cleanse your body from any type of thing that would cause that disease to get you. Believe God and live! Don't let these lies from Satan control your life!"

That's another reason people are oppressed. They come to Jesus and find forgiveness and freedom from their past sins, but Satan keeps whispering to them, "You're not really free. You're still going to suffer the consequences of all those things you've done in the past."

Friends, it's just not true. If Christ has set you free, you are free indeed.

When I am ministering to someone who is bothered by a spirit of oppression, I really try to knock it out of them. I make them look at me, and I make them listen to me, and sometimes I make them repeat after me words of power and release. And when they do repeat what I say, I make them repeat it with authority. I want them to hear themselves, and I want them to say it so forcefully that they can't help but believe it.

Oppression can be deadly. But it is no match for the power of Christ.

STEP NUMBER SIX IS OBSESSION

Now obsession is not necessarily bad. Some people are obsessed with the things of God, and that's a good way to be. If you're so obsessed with things of the Spirit that some people call you "a fool for Christ," you can feel very good about the life you're living.

But there is an evil form of obsession as well, and it can be a terrible and cruel taskmaster.

A person who is obsessed is one who is preoccupied with an idea or an emotion that cannot be broken by natural means. It is a persistent, inescapable preoccupation.

For example, surely you've heard about the young

woman who is obsessed with the idea that she is David Letterman's wife. Letterman himself says he never met the woman, but she is totally obsessed with him. She has broken into his house and done all sorts of things a normal person wouldn't do because of that obsession. She has been arrested, but that has not broken the hold this obsession has over her. She has been placed in jail...but that has not broken it. She has been publicly ridiculed and embarrassed, but that has not broken her obsession nor changed her behavior.

Admittedly, that's an unusual case. But it's an example of what obsession can do to a person. Usually, the obsessions that people develop are more "acceptable" in the eyes of the world. In other words, they don't cause headlines and hold people up to public ridicule — but they can be just as dangerous, just as deadly to the human spirit, and just as difficult to overcome.

For example, some people become obsessed with pornography. Others become obsessed with sex or sexual perversion. Some people become obsessed with the occult or new age teachings. Teenagers may become obsessed with rock or rap music. It's possible to be obsessed with money. Whatever you can think of, it's probably possible for someone to be obsessed with it.

It can start out innocently enough. A Christian businessman, on a trip and a long way from home, is flipping the channels on the television set in his hotel room — and there, on one of the channels is a sexually explicit movie. As soon as he sees what it is he changes the channel. But he can't get it out of his mind...and pretty soon he flips back to it, thinking that it won't hurt him to see what this is all about. After all, he tells himself, I'm just curious, and it's not like I'm really interested. Well, he sits there and watches the movie until it's over, and by the time it's over, he's hooked. He tries to turn away, but he can't.

That's how quickly an obsession can take control of you.

You have to be on guard against Satan's tricks. Don't think you're so strong that you would never fall into temptation.

You know, the Lord's prayer says, "Lead us not into temptation." It does not say, "Lead us into a temptation or two so we can resist it, and thereby show you how strong we are." Satan is doing his best to hit you where you are weakest, so pray that you will be able to avoid what he is throwing at you. Don't listen to what he wants to say to you. Don't look at what he wants you to see. He wants to hook you and reel you in, like a poor, obsessed, fish.

When you're obsessed with something, the only thing that happens, in the natural, is that you get in deeper and deeper, into more blatant types of sin.

What has happened to a person who is obsessed with some type of sinful behavior is that he has opened himself up to invasion by an evil spirit that is related to that desire. What happens in the case of obsession is that your desires become the demon's desires. And a devil is always obsessed with some sin or another.

For example, a person who is troubled by a lying spirit just will not be able to tell the truth. He's not lying to protect himself. He's not lying to avoid telling the truth about some painful issue. He's simply lying because that's all he can do. Ask him what day it is and he'll tell you Tuesday even though he knows it's Monday. Ask him for directions and he'll send you in the opposite direction from the way you really need to go. He is obsessed with lying.

Find a person who is troubled by a sex devil, and you'll find someone who just can't think about anything else. It will be all that person can think about, talk about, all he lives for.

You can see how terrible it is to be obsessed that way. The person who is a victim of one of these devils may try to shake it off at first. He tells himself that he's going to change, but he is totally powerless on his own. And those devilish fangs just sink deeper and deeper into his soul.

Pretty soon, he's reached the point where he doesn't see anything wrong with his behavior. He has lost the understanding of what is right and what is wrong. Unless the obsession is broken through God's divine power, this person is doomed.

There are several ways that an obsession can begin.

• Obsession can begin when you believe a lie.

"It won't hurt me to see just *one* X-rated movie." "I don't see anything wrong with having a few drinks." "I'm not doing anything wrong. Just flirting a little bit with my secretary."

One lie can lead to another. One improper step can be followed by other improper steps until you have strayed far from the proper path. Don't be taken in by any of the devil's lies. Instead, look to the Holy Spirit to guide you in every situation.

• Obsession can begin when you give in to jealousy.

For example, a husband decides that his wife is not to be trusted. She hasn't done anything wrong, really, but he has these nagging suspicions that just won't let go of him. He begins to question her in accusing tones about everything she does. "Where did you go today?" "What did you do?" "Who did you see?"

Pretty soon, two lives have all but been destroyed by the husband's obsessive jealousy.

Jealousy really is one of the devil's favorite tools. He loves to use it to cause strife among human beings. The "green-eyed monster" can break up marriages, family relationships, businesses, churches, you name it.

Be careful not to give in to jealousy. It can destroy you!

• Hatred can open the door to obsession.

As Christians, we're not allowed to hate anybody. Jesus told us that we are to love our enemies. I don't care what they've done, or how unlovable they might be, we still have to love them.

Sometimes, though, a Christian may find himself intensely disliking someone else in spite of himself. What you need to do, if you find that happening to you, is to pray for that person. Ask God to bless him or her. Ask God to help you see things from their point of view. Don't give in to the demons that want your heart to be full of hate.

Now some people have gotten into real trouble, not because they have hated others, but because they have assumed that others didn't like them. They think they're being excluded from things. They look for ways they've been slighted. They imagine that an innocent remark was a terrible insult.

When that begins to happen, you can be sure that there are demons in the air, whispering their lies: "Nobody likes you. They're all mean to you. You need to get even with them."

What those devils really want is to isolate and conquer you. Don't let it happen.

•Finally, obsession can come about through getting involved in some type of sin.

It is indulging in something you know is wrong, to the point where your willpower is totally gone. It's like what happens to a drug addict. When he first begins taking drugs, he tells himself that he only does it because it makes him feel good, and that he can stop anytime he wants to. But as time goes on, he begins to realize that that isn't really true. He gets to the point where he couldn't stop if his life depended on it — and sometimes it does.

For example, there is one major league baseball player who has been arrested and charged with possession of cocaine not once, not twice, not three times — but *seven* times. He's lost his marriage. He's very nearly lost his career. He has been banned from baseball for life and then reinstated. He has had warning after warning, and he has promised to get his life straightened out. But until now, he keeps going back to the drug. That's what can happen when a person begins to transgress God's laws.

Remember the old Chinese proverb which says, "A journey of 1,000 miles begins with one step." That's true of any journey, including the journey into the bondage and deception of obsession. If you want to maintain your freedom, don't ever take that first small step away from what you know is right.

POSSESSION

Now we have finally come to the seventh and last step along the road to demonic possession — and, in fact, that is possession itself. This is the final step in which the devil captures the immortal soul. There are demon possessed people all over the world, but most people that are bothered by devils are in one of the six other states we've discussed.

To be demon possessed means to be under absolute and total control of the devil. It means that your will power is owned by the spirit that lives in you. In some of the other cases we've been talking about demons may have been involved in the mind and the body, but not in the spirit. The person who is possessed has a demon or demons living within his spirit.

A person can become possessed when he fails to resist demonic attacks. For instance, suppose a lying spirit were attacking you, and you didn't resist him through the name and the blood of Jesus. That spirit would continue to work on you, night and day, until he was finally able to gain entrance into your spirit.

If you are a born-again spirit-filled Christian and you come into close proximity with someone who is demon possessed, that person will react to you in some way. It may be a major reaction or it may be a minor reaction.

There are some other ways you can tell if someone is possessed by a demon. For instance, this person may speak with a voice that is not human, or that is not their natural voice. A grown man may speak with the voice of a little boy, or a woman may speak with a man's deep bass voice. He or she may not even speak at all, but may bark like a dog or growl like some other animal. And then, sometimes their voice will change as they're talking to you — going from very high-pitched to very low-pitched and then back again in a matter of minutes.

I saw one case where the possessed person's tongue came out of her mouth like a snake, and made a clicking sound as it did. It wasn't hard to tell that this woman was in the hands of a demonic entity.

Sometimes you can even spot demon possession by the way a person carries himself. There's something about the way he walks, the way he holds his head and moves his arms. There's just something sinister about his body movements. Now I'm not saying that you should suspect anyone whose moves are a little "different" from normal. Just that there are certain characteristics that *can* indicate demonic involvement in someone's life.

Once a married couple came to me and asked if I could help their little boy, who was about 10 years old. They told me he would go into fits of terrible rage and anger, during which he would run through the house, destroying everything he could. He would smash mirrors, kick lamps onto the floor, throw furniture against the walls, etc. He would be sitting there being as nice and sweet as could be, and the next minute he was acting like a stark, raving mad lunatic.

These poor parents had taken their son to doctors and psychiatrists in an effort to help him, but nothing worked. Well, of course it hadn't worked. The little boy was possessed by a demon, and once it was cast out of him he was fine.

This is a common story. I am convinced that America's mental institutions are full of people who are not mentally ill at all, but who are possessed by demons. They don't need years and years of expensive psychiatric therapy. What they need is for someone to go in there in the power and authority of Jesus, and cast those demons out of them!

That's what you will see in church services when the Spirit of God really begins to move. Just as the anointing of the Holy Spirit is coming into the room, the devils will begin to scream and shout and do their best to disrupt things. When that happens, you need to move forward in Jesus' authority. Cast out those demons that are causing such trouble, and then get on with the celebration of God's presence and power!

To be possessed by an evil spirit is a terrible, terrible thing. It is the worst sort of bondage imaginable.

In our world today, there are thousands upon thousands of people who are trapped in that sort of bondage. They need to be set free, and they *can* be set free if Christians will move forward in the power and authority of Christ. I've said it before, but I need to say it again. There isn't a demon in the universe that can stand against the power of the Lord. In fact, all of the demons in the universe, including Lucifer himself, couldn't stand against the power of the Lord.

If you are living in the power of Christ, you have nothing at all to fear from demons. They have everything to fear from you.

In the next chapter, I'll tell you why demons fear you, and what you can do about it.

7

MOVING FORWARD IN THE POWER OF CHRIST

So far in this book, we've learned quite a bit about demons.

• We've found out where demons come from.

• We've talked about their leader, Lucifer, who is also known as Satan, and how he fell from heaven.

• We've seen that demons are the ones responsible for haunted houses, ghostly sightings, and are involved in many other occultic and new age practices such as seances, channeling, etc.

• We've seen how Christ dealt with demons.

• We've seen how the early church dealt with demons.

• And, we've seen how demons gain entrance into the human spirit.

That leaves one more very important matter to be discussed: How you can take authority over Satan and his armies from hell.

As I write this, I'm looking out my window on a clear, autumn evening, and I can see some of the lights of my neighborhood filtering through the trees. It's a clear night, with a beautiful full moon in the western sky. I can hear the droning of an airplane engine and see the lights blinking on and off as it passes overhead.

In other words, it's a normal night, and anyone who didn't know better would say that all is right with the world. Things are just the way they're supposed to be.

But that's not true.

There's a war raging out there. It's all around me — and all around you. Especially on this calm, clear night, it doesn't seem like there's a war in progress. But there is — and it's a war for control of every human being on this planet.

PRINCIPLE NUMBER ONE:
KNOW THAT YOU ARE IN A REAL WAR

Furthermore, it's a war to which we have all been summoned to fight. You are a soldier, and so am I. If you belong to Christ, you need to take this war, and your part in it, very seriously.

You need to be trained so that you not only can recognize the enemy, but can defeat him in hand-to-hand combat. And make no mistake about it. If you're ready and willing to be used, there will be plenty of hand-to-hand combat.

The first thing you need to know is that every Christian has been given a ministry of deliverance. We have all been called into this battle against the powers of darkness.

In Mark 16 verses 15-17, we find the part of the Scriptures known as The Great Commission. This is where Christ tells those who believe in Him to go into all of the world and preach the Gospel "to every living creature." I'm sure that every Bible-believing Christian would agree that this is important. But if you'll take a closer look at verse 17, you'll find these words:

"And these signs will accompany those who believe: In my name they will drive out demons..."

Who is Jesus talking about here? Those who believe. *All* those who believe. Do you believe in Jesus? Have you surrendered your life to Him? Is He your Lord and Savior? If so, he was talking about you. You should be driving out demons in His name.

I don't know how old you are. You may be 12, or you may be 102. It really doesn't matter, either, because you are never too young or too old to be a soldier in this war that rages throughout the entire cosmos. Some churches don't talk about deliverance at all. Some don't do it because they are embarrassed by the subject. Some don't do it because they're flat-out afraid of devils. And any church that is embarrassed of deliverance, or that is afraid of devils, is definitely going to *need* deliverance.

Don't be afraid. God has given you His power, but it's up to you to use it. And you should use it wherever and whenever its needed! Always remember that demons fear you because you are Christ's. The power of God is flowing through you, and that means that no demon can withstand you.

So again, the first principle in battling demons is to be aware of the fact that as a born-again believer, you have been called to cast out demons, and you have been given the power to do it.

PRINCIPLE NUMBER TWO: REMEMBER WHO YOU ARE IN JESUS

When you confront demons, they may tell you that they don't have to listen to you. They'll say that you're weak, and they may make reference to the fact that you're a sinner.

Your response to that needs to be that yes, they do have to listen to you, because you belong to Christ, and you are operating in His power and authority. Yes, it may be true that you are a weak human being, and that you are a sinner, because all human beings are sinners. But you have been justified and sanctified by the blood of Christ. When God looks at you, He does not see even the slightest smudge of sinful behavior. He sees only the righteousness that was given to you by His only begotten Son! When Christ ascended into Heaven, He gave us "weak" humans His name, which represents His victory and His capacity, and His ability to deal with any situation, including a confrontation with the worst demons hell has produced.

Use the name of Jesus. Demons don't want to hear it. It reminds them that they are defeated and doomed. That name gives you authority over *all* the powers of hell.

Sometimes the demons will talk to you and try to bargain with you. They'll tell you that they don't really mean any harm, and that they're not really demons, and do all sorts of things to try to trick you into leaving them alone. Don't listen. Don't be taken in. Cast them out by the authority that is yours in Christ.

Sometimes they will try to shock you. That's because they

realize that if they can break your concentration, and maybe even scare you a little bit, you'll back up and leave them alone. How will demons try to shock you? There are several ways. For example, the demon-possessed person will be talking in a human voice, and the next thing you know he's roaring like a lion or barking like a dog. Or the demon may cause his victim's body to go into strange contortions. It may be like in the movie, *The Exorcist*, where the demon-possessed girl kept vomiting up a substance that looked remarkably like pea soup! Whatever the demon may do, don't let it dissuade you from the task at hand. Remember who you are in Jesus, and cast that demon out.

Do you know who you are? You are an ambassador of the King of Kings. You are a new creature in Christ. You are an ambassador of New Jerusalem. You are the one God has sent to deliver this person from the grip of Satan. You are the one who has power over all the works of the devil. Do you understand all of this? Do you believe it? It's absolutely true. The power that created everything you see is resident within you. You're a frail little girl? You are a mighty warrior in Christ. You're a feeble old man? You, too, are a mighty warrior in Christ. I don't care if you're blind, or confined to a wheelchair, or if you have any other physical frailty or handicap. In Christ you are a warrior. In Christ, you will always be victorious over the forces of evil, just as the shepherd boy David was victorious over the mighty giant named Goliath.

You must face devils from your position and your authority. Don't come against them indecisively, trying to tiptoe around them somehow. You must face them as you would if you were a boxer, staring at your opponent across the other side of the ring.

They say that dogs can sense if a human is afraid of them. It's the same thing with demons. If they look at you and see that there is no fear in you, they will be afraid and know they are defeated.

PRINCIPLE THREE: PRAY IN TONGUES

Pray in tongues while you are casting out a demon. It helps to keep you alert and involved in the battle so that you are quickly aware when the devils try to trick you.

Now it could be that you are reading this, and you don't pray in tongues. If that's the case, it means that you have not been baptized with the Holy Spirit, and that's something you should seek. If you have not experienced the baptism with the Holy Spirit, you are not Spirit-filled and that means that you are not operating in the full capacity of spiritual strength God has available to you. Yes, you can be saved and not be baptized with the Holy Spirit. You can be living for Christ, and not be baptized with the Holy Spirit. But you are missing something important. Many good books have been written on this subject, and I strongly urge you to do some serious reading *and* praying.

Whenever I cast out demons, I pray in English and also in tongues. As I mentioned, praying in tongues helps me to be extra alert regarding what's going on, and that's important because the devil never runs out of tricks, and neither do his foot-soldiers.

For example, the demons may try to convince you that they've left their victim when they really haven't left at all. And if I've been praying in tongues, it helps me discern this, and keep on ordering them to leave until they're really gone.

Another thing that happens is that one or two demons, or perhaps even more, will actually be cast out of someone, but they'll leave more and stronger demons behind. Remember that a single human being may be the home of many demons. You're making a tragic mistake if you're quitting before the job is done — before the strongman inside of that person's spirit has been bound and cast out. But if you're praying in tongues and are tuned in, you'll *know* when the battle has been won. You will not be fooled.

PRINCIPLE FOUR: USE THE GIFTS OF THE SPIRIT

This cannot apply to you if you have not experienced the baptism with the Holy Ghost. And, again, if that's the case with you, then you are trying to fight demons without crucial weapons.

Many times when I have been casting out a demon, the Holy Spirit has given me a word of knowledge or a word of wisdom.

I will be able to say, "Look, you've had this problem, and that's what opened you up to demonic influences." The Lord may reveal to me that this person has had a problem with unforgiveness or unconfessed sin in his life.

Sometimes, I'll have to say, "You know, if you don't shut this door, and forgive this person, I can't cast this demon out," or "If you don't confess this sin to the Lord, I can't get rid of this thing."

It has been supernaturally revealed to me on more than one occasion that a person I was praying for had been opened up to demons as the result of being sexually abused as a child. The Holy Spirit also has allowed me to see that a lying spirit was given entrance into a person's spirit because abusive parents made him afraid to tell the truth about things when he was a child.

You can see how valuable that information is with regard to bringing total healing and freedom into that person's life.

I'm always happy when it is revealed to me how and why a demon was able to gain entrance into someone's life. It's great to be able to clear the demons out of a person's life, and it's also wonderful to be able to help them realize what changes they need to make — with the Lord's help — in order to prevent the return of those demons.

If the gifts of the Spirit are working in you, you'll know what to do in every situation. The same thing will happen to you if you are yielded to God, and operating in the power and direction of the Holy Spirit.

Now sometimes there is an anointing that will come upon you to deal with certain types of evil spirits or certain types of situations. It doesn't mean you can't deal with anything the devil throws at you, just that God has given you a special strength to deal with certain needs at that moment. Now I have found that such an anointing may not last all that long, so I want to make the most of it while I've got it.

For example, God may give me, for a brief period, a special anointing to deal with spirits that are linked to sexual perversion. If that's the case, I want to act on that, instead of spending my time casting out lying spirits, or spirits that are tied to things like unconfessed sin. Somebody says, "But aren't the people who are afflicted by those other kinds of demons just as important as those who are troubled by spirits of sexual perversion? Of course they are. But my point is that at this particular point in time, I have been given a special anointing to cast out those sex devils, and I must move in that anointing.

In my meetings, you will sometimes see me call for helpers to come and deal with certain types of demons. When I do that it's because I realize that a special type of anointing has been placed on me, and I don't want to step outside of that anointing to deal with other types of problems. And I know God well enough that I'm convinced He wouldn't give anybody a special anointing of any type if there wasn't an urgent need for it.

God is very economical, and He always does the thing that will do the most good for the most people. That's why it is so very important to follow His leading.

PRINCIPLE FIVE: ASK THEM IF THEY WANT TO BE FREE

What do I mean by this? Simply that some people don't want to be free, and even though it's possible to cast devils out of them, you may be wasting your time. Those devils will come right back and invade that person again because they know they're wanted.

Now there are some instances when people *can't* tell you that they want to be free because the demons within them won't let them tell you. And there are times when you just have to take authority, no matter what the person might say.

As a basic rule, if I find out that someone has demons because he invited them in, and that he doesn't really want to be rid of them, I'll just leave him alone.

Sometimes I'll ask questions like, "Do you want to live this perverted life? Do you really want this lifestyle?"

It could be that no one has ever asked a question like that before, and sometimes a puzzled answer will come back, "What do you mean?"

Then I have to get forceful: "I mean do you want to live in this state of mental derangement for the rest of your life, or do you want to be free and live a good life?"

If the answer comes, "I want to be free," I will ask, "Do you really mean that?" If they say they do, and I feel that they're telling the truth, then I will move right into deliverance — taking authority in the name of Jesus and casting that demon out.

PRINCIPLE SIX: HAVE FAITH IN THE NAME OF JESUS

There is tremendous power in the name of Jesus. But it is a power that is activated by faith in that name. Remember the story of the Jewish "exorcists" who tried to cast out demons, "in the name of Jesus whom Paul preaches." Instead of obeying their commands to come out of their victims, the demons reacted violently; the exorcists were fortunate to escape with their lives! They had no right to use the name of Jesus because they didn't believe in Him or His name. Therefore, it had no power for them.

You must believe whole-heartedly in Christ before you can use His name to cast out demons. Are you living for Him? Do you have a regular time to commune with Him daily? Do you study and meditate upon the Word of God to the point where it is down inside of you where you can draw upon it when you need it? Do you understand and believe in the power of the Word of God?

If you don't have faith that what the Word says is true, you can quote it to demons all day long, and they'll just stay in there and yawn. They won't care. If it doesn't have any meaning to you, it won't have any meaning to them when you try to use it.

When you say, "In the name of Jesus, come out of that person," you have to understand that the name you're using is the name above all names. It is the name that will cause every living creature to bow in complete reverence and worship. The blessed, holy, wonderful name of Jesus! When you use the name of Jesus that way, it is like a bomb going off to hit that evil force and knock it out of the way.

PRINCIPLE SEVEN: DON'T BE NERVOUS

Yes, I understand that you're bound to be a bit nervous the first time you step forward in faith to cast out devils. But ask God to help you move out in boldness and faith and to take away the nervousness you feel, and He will do it. It is so important that you learn to stay as peaceful as possible, concentrating on the glory and power of Christ.

I have had experiences where it seemed like a full-scale battle was raging all around me. People were crawling around the floor, slithering like snakes, others were growling or barking, or whining and crying. Yet in the middle of it, I felt a great peacefulness. That is the peace that passes understanding, and it is available to you as a child of God.

It's not always the demons that make you nervous. Sometimes, you may be surprised by the person you're praying for. What I mean is that I have seen prayer lines where respected community and church leaders have come forward, and it quickly becomes apparent that there is deep-rooted demonic involvement in their lives. The natural tendency would be to say something like, "Oh, I can't believe it! *You*, troubled by demons?"

Well, don't worry about it. Just cast that demon out and then go on with your life. Always remember that deliverance has not been given so that you can judge people. It has been given so you can set people free. Sometimes, people who are respected in a community or church don't get the help they need because they are embarrassed. Pride is what keeps them bound. So when you find yourself ministering deliverance to someone you have looked up to and respected, don't be nervous, and don't let it diminish the way you feel about that person. Just get him or her free, and praise God that He is using you as a conduit for His power.

And that brings me to another important point. Don't talk about the experience after it's over. It's true that immediately after the demon has been cast out, you may have to talk to the person and explain what has happened — just to make sure they follow it and that they realize they've been set free by the power of Jesus. But once you've done that, let it go and forget about it.

Now if you do it in the right attitude, it can be a good idea to occasionally check up on someone who has been set free. That means it's okay just to drop by and ask how they're doing. Have they experienced any problems. Have there been any demonic attacks? If so, then ask the person to pray with you, and ask the Lord to continue to protect and minister to them. Remind the devil, together, that you have cast him out and that he has no authority over this person. Then, remind the person how to take authority over the forces of evil when they attack him. Remind him that he doesn't have to listen to them, and that if he resists them in the Name of Jesus, they will flee. Always remember that your time together and your conversation is confidential. It should remain between the two of you, so don't share it with anyone else. To be blunt about it, it is nobody else's business.

Don't go around the church telling everyone you know that you just cast a demon out of Old So-And-So. And don't walk up to Old So-And-So every time you see him after that and say, "Remember that time I cast the demon out of you?" No good purpose is served by that kind of behavior. What has happened has happened, so let it go, and move on into the future.

It is possible to be flowing in the Spirit to the point where you may not even remember afterwards who it was you were dealing with. I have had people come up to me and say, "Remember me...I'm the one you cast that demon out of last week?" And I'll have to apologize and say, "No, I'm sorry, but I really don't remember you at all." I don't want to hurt anyone's feelings, but the truth is that, when I'm in a large service, and numbers of people are coming forward for healing or deliverance, I'm operating in the power of the Spirit. The Holy Spirit is working through me to the point that I sometimes won't remember things I've said or done, moments after I've said or done them!

PRINCIPLE EIGHT: THERE IS POWER IN THE LAYING-ON OF HANDS

Don't be afraid to put your hands on the demon-possessed person. When the power of God is flowing through you, it will flow right out of your hands into the body of the person you're ministering to.

Read the New Testament, and you'll find that the Holy Spirit was often given by the laying on of the Apostles' hands. There is a spiritual principle at work here, so use it.

Sometimes, when you have your hands on the body of a victim of possession, you will feel that evil spirit moving through them. For example, I have had my hands on someone's stomach, and I can feel the demon moving upward, through the chest, the throat, and finally out the mouth. There is a demonic knot, or mass, that can actually be felt moving through the body on its way out. Often, people will begin to choke as the demon moves through the throat. I've had people start to cry and panic, "I can't breathe! I'm choking! I'm going to die!"

Whenever that happens, I tell them to calm down, that the demon is in the process of leaving the body, and that they are not going to die. Instead, they are going to live...and live in a joyous freedom they have not known before.

So again, practice the laying on of hands. If you are living for God, your hands belong to Him, and He wants to let His power flow through them.

Those then, are eight important principles for dealing with demons. To recap, they are:

1) Understand that you have been called to cast out demons and that you have the power and authority to do it.

2) Know who you are in Jesus.

3) Before ministering to a person, ask him if he wants to be set free.

4) Have faith in the name of Jesus and the Word of God.

5) Don't be nervous.

6) Pray in tongues.

7) Seek and use the gifts of the Spirit.

8) Practice the laying-on of hands.

Remember that at the start of this chapter, I told you that there is a war raging in the universe. It is absolutely true. Now I want you to understand that the outcome has already been decided. It's like the old preacher said, "I've looked in the back of the Book, and guess what? We win!"

Yes, we're going to win — glory to God!

But even though the devil doesn't have a single chance to be victorious, he is still intent on causing as many casualties as he possibly can. The outcome of the war has been determined, but vicious and bloody fighting continues. Satan continues his indiscriminate attacks on people of all ages, races, and lifestyles.

We've got to stop him and his armies. We've got to fight back. God has given us absolute power over the forces of darkness. He commands us to advance against the enemy. Every one of us!

The time has come to go forth and conquer — in the mighty name of Jesus!

Additional copies of this book are available from your local bookstore or by contacting:

Embassy Publishing
P.O. Box 3500, Laguna Hills, CA 92654

Roberts Liardon Ministries International Offices:

In England, Europe, Eastern Europe, and Scandanavia
P.O. Box 103
Knutsford
Cheshire WA169EL
England

In Asia:
Roberts Liardon
Raffles City
P.O. Box 1365
Singapore 9117

In New Zealand and Australia:
Lifeway Ministries
P.O. Box 303
Warkworth, New Zealand

Other Books by Roberts Liardon

Run to the Battle
Learning To Say No Without Feeling Guilty
Kathryn Kuhlman
A Spiritual Biography of God's Miracle Working Power
I Saw Heaven
A Call to Action
The Invading Force
The Quest for Spiritual Hunger
Religious Politics
Breaking Controlling Powers
Cry of the Spirit
Spiritual Timing
The Price of Spiritual Power
How to Survive An Attack
What Jesus Likes to do Through You
Final Approach

Videos by Roberts Liardon

I Saw Heaven
God's Explosive Weapons
The Roar of the '90s
The Sword of Gideon
Developing an Excellent Spirit
No More Walls
Confronting the Brazen Heavens
Invasion '91 (10-tape series)
Reformers and Revivalists (5-volume series)
God's Generals
(8-volume set of tapes, 60 minutes each)

To contact Roberts Liardon
write:

Roberts Liardon Ministries
P.O. Box 30710, Laguna Hills, CA 92654

Please include your prayer requests and comments when you write.

REVIVAL TO THE NATIONS

A NEW GENERATION BRINGING REVIVAL TO THE NATIONS

Spirit Life Bible College
Laguna Hills, California

I t is the heart of Spirit Life Bible College to raise and train a generation of people to go out and subdue the hardened spiritual climate of a nation, and win it for the Kingdom of God. We will train our students how to live victoriously in any environment, emerging with the message, the joy and the life of God.

Roberts Liardon
Founder & President

Some of the courses include:

Spiritual Leadership	God's Generals
Gifts of the Spirit	Human Illness & Healing
Soul Development/The Mind of Christ	
Spiritual Timing	Spirit of Revival
Dynamics of Faith	The Champions of God
The Ministry Gifts	Roots of Character
and much, much more!	

You have a part — isn't it time you did something to reach the world for Jesus Christ? Send today for your application and catalog!

For more information or to receive a catalog and an application, please call (714) 751-1700 or write:

Roberts Liardon Ministries
P.O. Box 30710
Laguna Hills, CA 92654-0710

Discounts for couples and child care available

Order Form

VIDEOS

Prod. #	Qty.	Titles
VL-CB-HE		"Confronting the Brazen Heavens" ......NEW $19.95
VL-DE-SP		"Developing an Excellent Spirit" $19.95
VL-GE-WP		"God's Explosive Weapons" $19.95

"GOD'S GENERALS — The Healing Evangelists"

Prod. #	Qty.	Titles
GG-001-00		(Complete 8 Volume Video Series) $159.60
GG-01-08		"Vol. 1 Intro./John Alexander Dowie" $19.95
GG-02-08		"Vol. 2 Maria Woodworth-Etter/ Evan Roberts" $19.95
GG-03-08		"Vol. 3 Charles F. Parham/John G. Lake"......$19.95
GG-04-08		"Vol. 4 William 'Daddy' Seymour/ Aimee Semple McPherson"........................$19.95
GG-05-08		"Vol. 5 Smith Wigglesworth/ William Branham"..............................$19.95
GG-06-08		"Vol. 6 Jack Coe" (Parts 1&2)........................$19.95
GG-07-08		"Vol. 7 Kathryn Kuhlman" (Parts 1&2)......$19.95
GG-08-08		"Vol. 8 A. A. Allen/Conclusion" $19.95

CONTINUATION OF GOD'S GENERALS

Prod. #	Qty.	Titles
RR-00-00		Reformers & Revivalists (5 Volume Series)........$100.00
RR-01-05		Vol. 1 M. Luther/ J. Knox/ G. Fox................$20.00
RR-02-05		Vol. 2 J. Edwards/ G. Whitfield $20.00
RR-03-05		Vol. 3 J. Wesley/ C. Finney..........................$20.00
RR-04-05		Vol. 4 P. Cartwright/ Cain Ridge Campmtng $20.00
RR-05-05		Vol. 5 D.L. Moody/ C. Spurgeon.................$20.00
VI-91-00		INVASION (10 Volume Series)...........$200.00
VI-91-01		#1 Roberts Liardon – "Spirit of Evan." $20.00
VI-91-02		#2 Rod Parsley – "The Subject of Sin" $20.00
VI-91-03		#3 "Gram" Moore – "Seeking God"................$20.00
VI-91-04		#4 Benny Hinn – "The Anointing"...............$20.00
VI-91-05		#5 Roberts Liardon – "A New Nation"..........$20.00
VI-91-06		#6 Lester Sumrall – "Missionary Vision".............$20.00
VI-91-07		#7 John Mason – "God's Gift in You"..............$20.00
VI-91-08		#8 Morris Cerullo – "A God of Purpose"..........$20.00
VI-91-09		#9 Ulf Christiansson – "Power of the Gospel".......$20.00
VI-91-10		#10 Roberts Liardon – "A New Generation" $20.00
VL-IS-HE		"I Saw Heaven" $19.95
VL-NM-WL		"No More Walls".................................$19.95
VL-RO-90		"The Roar of the '90s"........................$19.95
VL-GM-SG		"The Sword of Gideon" (By Roberts grandmother Gladoylene Moore)........ $19.95

TAPE ALBUMS

Prod. #	Qty.	Titles
AS-RL-01		"Answering the Deep" (2 tapes) $10.00
AS-RL-19		"Apostles, Prophets & Terr. Churches" (6 tapes)...NEW $30.00
AS-RL-02		"How To Live A Strong Life" (3 tapes)......$15.00
AS-RL-09		"Changing Spiritual Climates" $20.00
AS-RL-26		"Doors of Utterance" (4 tapes) ....NEW $20.00
AS-RL-10		"God's Explosive Weapons" (4 tapes).....$20.00
AS-RL-11		"Habitation vs. Visitation" (4 tapes)...............$20.00
AS-RL-03		"Harnessing The Human Will" (2 tapes)......$10.00
AS-RL-12		"How To Survive an Attack" (4 tapes)...........$20.00
AS-RL-23		Invasion '91 Conference (15 tapes) $59.00
AS-RL-24		Invasion '92 Conference (15 tapes)..............$69.00
AS-RL-08		"Life & Ministry of Kath. Kuhlman" (3 tapes)..$15.00
AS-RL-13		"Living on the Offensive" (4 tapes) $20.00
AS-RL-04		"Personality of the Holy Spirit" (2 tapes) $10.00
AS-RL-18		Reformers & Revivalists (5 tapes) $25.00
AS-GM-01		"Rivers of Living Water" by Gladoylene Moore, Roberts' grandmother (2 tapes) $10.00
AS-RL-14		"School of the Spirit" (4 tapes) $20.00
AS-RL-05		"Taking a City" (2 tapes) $10.00
AS-RL-22		Tape of the Month Club 1992 ....$58.00
AS-RL-20		"The Best of Roberts Liardon" (6 tapes)......$30.00
AS-RL-21		"The Healing Evangelists" (8 tapes)...........$40.00
AS-RL-15		"The Prophet's Office" (4 tapes) $20.00
AS-RL-06		"True Spiritual Strength" (2 tapes) $10.00
AS-RL-25		"Useable Faith" (6 tapes) ....NEW $30.00
AS-RL-16		"Victorious Living in the Last Days" (4 tapes) ...$20.00
AS-RL-07		"You Need the Spirit of Might and Power" (2 Tapes) ..$10.00
AS-RL-17		"Your Faith Stops the Devil" (4 tapes) $20.00

SINGLE TAPES

Prod. #	Qty.	Titles
AC-RL-16		"A Valiant Generation" $5.00
AC-RL-14		"Almost Christian" $5.00
AC-RL-17		"Becoming Spiritually Fit" $5.00
AC-RL-02		"Building Your Ark in the Spirit" $5.00
AC-RL-08		"Developing an Excellent Spirit" $5.00
AC-RL-06		"Don't Let the Devil Destroy Your Purpose" $5.00
AC-RL-20		"Faith that Subdues" $5.00
AC-RL-22		"Forget Not His Benefits"..............................$5.00
AC-RL-10		"God's Clock Is Ticking" $5.00
AC-RL-19		"Holding to the Word of the Lord" $5.00
AC-RL-05		"How To Be Fervent".....................................$5.00
AC-RL-11		"I Saw Heaven" $5.00
AC-RL-12		"Knowing People By the Spirit" $5.00
AC-RL-21		"Obey Your Heavenly Call" $5.00
AC-RL-13		"Progression Breaks Regression"..................$5.00
AC-RL-03		"Raising the Healing Banner of Christ" $5.00
AC-RL-07		"Return to Intercession and Deliverance" $5.00
AC-RL-15		"Stirring Up the Gifts of God" $5.00
AC-RL-01		"The Calling Voice of God" $5.00
AC-RL-09		"The Glory of the Young Is Their Strength" $5.00
AC-RL-18		"The Manifestation of the Holy Spirit" $5.00
AC-RL-04		"The Spiritual Operation of Laying on of Hands".....................................$5.00

BOOKS

Prod. #	Qty.	Titles
BO3-12-0		A Call to Action $5.99
BO3-09-0		Breaking Controlling Powers........................$5.99
BO3-10-4		Cry of the Spirit – Smith Wigglesworth.....$7.99
BO3-14-7		Forget Not His Benefits ....NEW $5.99
BO3-15-5		Haunted Houses, Ghosts & Demons ......NEW $5.99
BO3-00-7		How to Survive An Attack (112 pages)........$5.95
BO3-11-2		I Saw Heaven $3.99
BO3-08-2		Kathryn Kuhlman $7.99
BO3-05-8		Learning To Say NO $3.99
BO3-02-3		Religious Politics ....$ .98
BO3-06-6		Run to the Battle $6.99
BO3-07-4		Spiritual Timing $3.99
BO-338-1		The Final Approach ....NEW $7.99
BO3-03-1		The Invading Force $3.99
BO3-04-X		The Price of Spiritual Power $2.99
BO3-13-9		The Quest For Spiritual Hunger $2.99
BO3-01-5		What Jesus Likes To Do Through You ...NEW $3.99

Product Total _____

Postage & Handling _____

Sub Total _____

Offering _____

California residents please add 7.75% Tax _____

TOTAL _____

☐ Please send information about **Revivalists Research Center** and your list of available books and tapes

☐ I want to be a *Spirit Life International Partner* with you in your ministry, and I will support you with a monthly love gift of $_____.

☐ Enclosed is my one-time gift of $_____.

☐ Please send me information about **Spirit Life Bible College.**

*NOTE: ALL PRICES PAYABLE IN U.S. DOLLARS

Order Form

Mail This Coupon or Rush Order by Credit Card, Call: (714) 751-1700

☐ Please charge my order to my: ☐ Master Card ☐ Visa

CARD NO.

☐☐☐☐☐☐☐☐☐☐☐☐☐☐☐☐☐☐☐

EXP. DATE ☐☐☐☐

MO. ☐☐ YR. ☐☐

Signature _____

Name *(Print)* _____

Phone # _____

Address _____

City _____

State _____ Zip _____

UPS available for additional charge:
☐ UPS Std.   ☐ UPS next Day   ☐ UPS 2nd Day   ☐ UPS 3rd Day

POSTAGE AND HANDLING

$1.00-$5.00 purchase ....Add $1.25

$5.01-$15.00 purchase ....Add $2.50

$15.01-$25.00 purchase ....Add $3.50

$25.01-$50.00 purchase ....Add $5.00

$50.01-$100.00 purchase ....Add $6.00

Over $100.00 ....Free Shipping

Please return any defective merchandise and Roberts Liardon Ministries will replace within the first 30 days of purchase. Prices are subject to change without notice. Prices effective through 12/31/93.

FOREIGN ORDERS RESPONSIBLE FOR ADDITIONAL POSTAGE.

CALL OUR OFFICE FOR A QUOTE.

Roberts Liardon Ministries
P.O. Box 30710, Laguna Hills, CA 92654-0710

(714) 751-1700
Fax: (714) 751-0808